DATE DUE		

COMPREHENSIVE RESEARCH
AND STUDY GUIDE

William Carlos
Williams

BLOOM'S
MAJOR
POETS

EDITED AND WITH AN INTRODUCTION
BY HAROLD BLOOM

CURRENTLY AVAILABLE

BLOOM'S MAJOR DRAMATISTS	BLOOM'S MAJOR NOVELISTS	BLOOM'S MAJOR POETS	BLOOM'S MAJOR SHORT STORY WRITERS
Aeschylus	Jane Austen	Maya Angelou	Jorge Louis Borges
Aristophanes	The Brontës	Elizabeth Bishop	Italo Calvino
Berthold Brecht	Willa Cather	William Blake	Raymond Carver
Anton Chekhov	Stephen Crane	Gwendolyn Brooks	Anton Chekhov
Henrik Ibsen	Charles Dickens	Robert Browning	Joseph Conrad
Ben Johnson	William Faulkner	Geoffrey Chaucer	Stephen Crane
Christopher Marlowe	F. Scott Fitzgerald	Sameul Taylor Coleridge	William Faulkner
Arthur Miller	Nathaniel Hawthorne	Dante	F. Scott Fitzgerald
Eugene O'Neill	Ernest Hemingway	Emily Dickinson	Nathaniel Hawthorne
Shakespeare's Comedies	Henry James	John Donne	Ernest Hemingway
Shakespeare's Histories	James Joyce	H.D.	O. Henry
Shakespeare's Romances	D. H. Lawrence	T. S. Eliot	Shirley Jackson
Shakespeare's Tragedies	Toni Morrison	Robert Frost	Henry James
George Bernard Shaw	John Steinbeck	Seamus Heaney	James Joyce
Neil Simon	Stendhal	Homer	Franz Kafka
Oscar Wilde	Leo Tolstoy	Langston Hughes	D.H. Lawrence
Tennessee Williams	Mark Twain	John Keats	Jack London
August Wilson	Alice Walker	John Milton	Thomas Mann
	Edith Wharton	Sylvia Plath	Herman Melville
	Virginia Woolf	Edgar Allan Poe	Flannery O'Connor
		Poets of World War I	Edgar Allan Poe
		Shakespeare's Poems & Sonnets	Katherine Anne Porter
		Percy Shelley	J. D. Salinger
		Alfred, Lord Tennyson	John Steinbeck
		Walt Whitman	Mark Twain
		William Carlos Williams	John Updike
		William Wordsworth	Eudora Welty
		William Butler Yeats	

COMPREHENSIVE RESEARCH
AND STUDY GUIDE

William Carlos

Williams

EDITED AND WITH AN INTRODUCTION
BY HAROLD BLOOM

First Printing
1 3 5 7 9 8 6 4 2

Library of Congress Cataloging-in-Publication Data
William Carlos Williams / Harold Bloom, ed..
        p. cm. —(Bloom's major poets)
    Includes bibliographical references and index.
    ISBN 0-7910-6814-5
    1. Williams, William Carlos, 1883–1963—Criticism and.
    interpretation.
    I. Series.
PS3545 .I544 2002
    811'.52—dc21   2002003963

Chelsea House Publishers
1974 Sproul Road, Suite 400
Broomall, PA 19008-0914

http://www.chelseahouse.com

Contributing Editor: Gabriel Welsch

Layout by EJB Publishing Services

CONTENTS

USER'S GUIDE

This volume is designed to present biographical, critical, and biblio-graphical information on the author and the author's best-known or most important poems. Following Harold Bloom's editor's note and introduction is a concise biography of the author that discusses major life events and important literary accomplishments. A critical analysis of each poem follows, tracing significant themes, patterns, and motifs in the work. As with any study guide, it is recommended that the reader read the poem beforehand and have a copy of the poem being discussed available for quick reference.

A selection of critical extracts, derived from previously published material, follows each thematic analysis. In most cases, these extracts represent the best analysis available from a number of leading critics. Because these extracts are derived from previously published material, they will include the original notations and references when available. Each extract is cited, and readers are encouraged to check the original publication as they continue their research. A bibliography of the author's writings, a list of additional books and articles on the author and their work, and an index of themes and ideas conclude the volume.

ABOUT THE EDITOR

Harold Bloom is Sterling Professor of the Humanities at Yale University and Henry W. and Albert A. Berg Professor of English at the New York University Graduate School. He is the author of over 20 books, and the editor of more than 30 anthologies of literary criticism.

Professor Bloom's works include *Shelly's Mythmaking* (1959), *The Visionary Company* (1961), *Blake's Apocalypse* (1963), *Yeats* (1970), *A Map of Misreading* (1975), *Kabbalah and Criticism* (1975), *Agon: Toward a Theory of Revisionism* (1982), *The American Religion* (1992), *The Western Canon* (1994), and *Omens of Millennium: The Gnosis of Angels, Dreams, and Resurrection* (1996). *The Anxiety of Influence* (1973) sets forth Professor Bloom's provocative theory of the literary relationships between the great writers and their predecessors. His most recent books include *Shakespeare: The Invention of the Human*, a 1998 National Book Award finalist, *How to Read and Why* (2000), and *Stories and Poems for Extremely Intelligent Children of All Ages* (2001).

Professor Bloom earned his Ph.D. from Yale University in 1955 and has served on the Yale faculty since then. He is a 1985 MacArthur Foundation Award recipient and served as the Charles Eliot Norton Professor of Poetry at Harvard University in 1987–88. In 1999 he was awarded the prestigious American Academy of Arts and Letters Gold Medal for Criticism. Professor Bloom is the editor of several other Chelsea House series in literary criticism, including BLOOM'S MAJOR SHORT STORY WRITERS, BLOOM'S MAJOR NOVELISTS, BLOOM'S MAJOR DRAMATISTS, MODERN CRITICAL INTERPRETATIONS, MODERN CRITICAL VIEWS, and BLOOM'S BIOCRITIQUES.

EDITOR'S NOTE

My Introduction centers on the lyric, "By the road to the contagious hospital," from *Spring and All*. That remarkable lyric is seen by David Walker as a juxtaposition or balance of contraries, a reading consonant with Peter Schmidt's remarks upon Biblical allusions, and with John Lowney's reflections on rebirth in Williams.

Paul Mariani locates the source of "The Yachts" in Dante's *Inferno*, while "The Wanderer" is rightly judged by Richard Macksey as William's movement into a post-Imagist mode.

"Burning the Christmas Greens" is celebrated by Roy Harvey Pearce as an emergence into Williams's major mode, after which "January Morning" is usefully compared by John Lowney to Whitman's "Crossing Brooklyn Ferry."

"These," where the central difficulty may be perspective, is illuminated by the remarks of Janet Sullivan.

Harold Bloom

In my youth and middle years, I rendered scarce critical justice to Williams, though I read his best poetry with continuous pleasure, finding in him a superb fusion of the very different legacies of John Keats and of Walt Whitman. My problem was not so much with Williams as with his extravagant exegetes, some of them my dear friends, like Hollis Miller and the much-missed Joseph Riddel. Literalizing Williams's own drum-beatings, his devoted admirers gave us a poet who had broken through, beyond metaphysics, into a new realm of being. Palpably, no poet—not Wordsworth nor Whitman—has done that since Shakespeare, and Williams was ill-served by such critical inflation.

Now, almost forty years since the death of Williams, it may be possible to see him more plainly. His gift for language was astonishing, yet his mind was commonplace. He was not a master of nuance, like Whitman, and like his own contemporaries, Wallace Stevens and T. S. Eliot. Nor did he have the incantatory power of Hart Crane, a poet he deprecated, who still caused him considerable anxiety. I prefer him to Ezra Pound, whose cadences deeply influenced the style of *Paterson*, Williams's major work, but then Pound, a great sensibility, destroyed his own poetry with the sickness of anti-Semitism. Perhaps Williams's eminence is roughly comparable to that of Marianne Moore, in his own generation. Like her, he composed extraordinary poems, but (at least to me) something less than a whole canon of works, marked by significant variety and power of mind. Unlike Frost and Stevens, Eliot and Hart Crane, Williams—in my judgment—falls just short of the American Sublime of Walt Whitman and Emily Dickinson.

Despite such reservations, I am overcome by Williams at his strongest, as in the visionary lyric, "By the Road to the contagious hospital" in *Spring and All* (1923). An extraordinary energy drives the poem's opening:

> **By the road to the contagious hospital**
> under the surge of the blue
> mottled clouds driven from the

northeast—a cold wind. Beyond, the
waste of broad, muddy fields
brown with dried weeds, standing and fallen

patches of standing water
the scattering of tall trees

All along the road the reddish
purplish, forked, upstanding, twiggy
stuff of bushes and small trees
with dead, brown leaves under them
leafless vines—

Lifeless in appearance, sluggish
dazed spring approaches—

A harsh splendor in a hard spring comprises three kinds of rebirth:
grass and leaves, human infants, post-Whitmanian American poems.
Dr. Williams, who had delivered innumerable babies, utilizes the
authority of his experience with a memorable eloquence:

They enter the new world naked,
cold, uncertain of all
save that they enter. All about them,
the cold, familiar wind—

Now the grass, tomorrow
the stiff curl of wildcarrot leaf

One by one objects are defined—
It quickens: clarity, outline of leaf

But now the stark dignity of
entrance—Still, the profound change
has come upon them: rooted, they
grip down and begin to awaken

How can one overpraise this? The "new world" is at once spring,
fresh human life, and the poems of our climate, as Stevens called
them. Here, at his very best, Williams helped make the world new.

William Carlos Williams

William Carlos Williams is now widely recognized as one of the most important poets of the twentieth century, specifically of the period between the two world wars. Typically, he is invoked when critics discuss the Modernist movement, and he is associated with such luminaries as T.S. Eliot, Ezra Pound, Wallace Stevens, Robert Frost, and Marianne Moore. However, he has not always enjoyed such a favorable critical reputation. It was not until very late in his life and career that he began to appear in definitive anthologies. Practically no scholarly work of any sort appears on Williams prior to 1955. What few mentions there are mostly dismiss Williams as less innovative and less cerebral than his contemporaries.

William Carlos Williams was born on September 17, 1883 in Rutherford, New Jersey, an industrial suburb of New York City near the Passaic River in northeastern New Jersey. He came from a mixed background; his grandmother had lived for a time in Puerto Rico with her second husband. His mother, Raquel, was from Puerto Rico and his father was English. However, the larger family had Jewish, Dutch, and Basque backgrounds. Thus, while Williams was not as traveled as many of his contemporaries, he felt he possessed an inner awareness of the world as a result of his varied background.

Williams attended the University of Pennsylvania, initially for dentistry. However, shortly after his arrival he switched to medicine. His father had been a traveling salesman for a perfume company, and Williams himself sought means of employment that would not take him far from home. Still, while at Penn he continued his attempts at painting and writing. At the same time, he met Ezra Pound and Hilda Doolittle, and thus began what would become important lifelong friendships that would have a profound influence on his writing.

On graduating from medical school, Williams traveled to Leipzig, Germany, for a brief residency before returning to the states. During his time there, he traveled throughout Western Europe while under-taking advance training in pediatrics, which would become the spe-cialty of his general practice. (Williams is credited with delivering over 2000 babies.) He returned to the states and married Florence

Herman (Flossie) in 1912, after several years of courting. While he had paid to have his first collection, *Poems*, published in 1909, he had spent the intervening years trying to get his practice established in Rutherford. He had dreams of involving himself in the literary and artistic world, but saw to the task of his practice first. The resulting devotion to two careers has earned Williams frequent comparisons to Chekhov. Like Chekhov, Williams was known for making house calls, being available, knowing his patients personally, all of which earned him the affectionate designation as an "old-fashioned doc." But Williams, unlike Chekhov, was not a rural doctor. Williams saw to the poor and working families of two industrial towns that were growing into cities. The job was exhausting, even without attempting to lead a second career.

But he did. Once his practice was firmly established, he began to pursue his writing career in more earnest. He gained particular drive after the famous Armory Show of 1913. The same year, his second collection of poems, *The Tempers*, was published. He had still not broken the ground stylistically and thematically that would make him famous, but he was headed toward it. He and Flossie spent weekends in New York and during that period he came to know Alfred Kreymborg, Marianne Moore, Wallace Stevens, Marcel Duchamp, Maxwell Bodenheim, and Edna St. Vincent Millay. With Moore and Stevens in particular Williams maintained critical, lasting, and, with Stevens, often contentious friendships.

Between 1917 and 1925, Williams published the experimental and thematically groundbreaking works in prose and poetry that would define his early aesthetic and lay the foundation for his later, far more complex works. In that period, he published the poetry collection *Al Que Quiere!*, the prose experiment *Kora in Hell: Improvisations*; the collection of Imagist lyrics *Sour Grapes*; *The Great American Novel*; the experimental sequence *Spring and All*; *GO GO*; and what many consider his early philosophical statement, *In the American Grain*.

Despite his interest and participation in the changing literary and artistic landscape, Williams did not travel abroad. The only exception was when he visited Flossie and his two sons while they were vacationing in Europe. He met them in London in 1924, and at the same time first met James Joyce. He kept correspondence with many writers and artists living in Europe, notably H.D. and Robert McAlmon, with whom Williams co-edited the influential small magazine *Contact.*

Throughout the late 1920s and early 1930s, Williams continued to write stories, plays, novels, autobiographies while running his practice and raising a family with Flossie. Critics point out that his work became darker during the period, and he struggled increasingly with the aesthetic question of how to merge and divide poetry and prose. He wrote his early poem "Paterson" in 1927, and the idea of mining that place haunted him increasingly in those years. According to Linda Wagner-Martin, the short 1944 collection *The Wedge* (the first to be published after 1938's *The Complete Collected Poems*) showed the weariness and demands that the war and the escalating demands of his patients had on him. Shortly afterward, his writing was rejuvenated as he set down the beginnings of the epic *Paterson*. Book I appeared in 1946, stating clearly on its first page the philosophy he had long adhered to and yet seldom articulated so well: "No ideas but in things."

The first book was a daring piece comprised of snippets taken from the surroundings and documentary history of Paterson: stark images reminiscent of Williams' early works, sketches of actual residents and patients, newspaper clippings, public documents, and the like, interspersed with prose and highly experimental passages of verse. In among the tumult was a now famous fan-letter from one of Williams' admirers, known in the book only as A.G. It was the then unknown Beat poet Allen Ginsburg. In 1955, Williams wrote the introduction for Ginsberg's *Howl and Other Poems.*

The other books in the series followed every few years. During that time Williams also began to see the first results of a nascent appreciation for his work. In 1947 he taught briefly at the University of Washington. The following year he was able to work at Yaddo, the only time in his life he was ever afforded a long period of time to focus on literary work. However, despite the small reprieve he was afforded from his grueling schedule, he had been at it for almost thirty years, it had taken a toll. In 1948, he suffered a heart attack, and in 1951, a stroke. He left his medical practice for his sons to oversee. Nonetheless, he had two more strokes in 1952 and 1953. It was a bittersweet time. As his health was ailing, his reputation grew. In

1950 he won the National Book Award for *Selected Poems* and *Paterson III*, and Random House started to publish his work. The indicators were that he had become accepted by the mainstream intellectual community.

There were still some problems. During the furor of the McCarthy hearings, when some of Williams' associations with the far left came to light, he was denied the post of consultant in poetry to the Library of Congress (the forerunner of the position known today as the United States Poet Laureate). He was also hospitalized for depression during part of 1953. Despite winning the Bollingen Prize for Poetry in 1953 (which he shared with Archibald MacLeish) Williams nonetheless felt that all he had done in his work to make American ideas and American landscapes and people a central and relevant aspect of literature was futile in the face of the country's destructive politics at the time.

In 1955, a fourth stroke left Williams partially paralyzed. He had to relearn how to type and how to speak. After which he was able to finish *Paterson*, write a biography of his mother, and to put together a final collection of poetry, *Pictures from Brueghel and other poems*. William Carlos Williams died on March 4, 1963, in Rutherford, and was awarded the Pulitzer Prize posthumously for his 1962 work *Pictures from Brueghel and Other Poems*.

"Spring and All"

Spring and All is the title of what is perhaps William's most famous sequence of poems, not including *Paterson*. The entire sequence was first published in 1923 by Contact Editions in Paris, the press owned and operated by Robert McAlmon; the press was an outgrowth of *Contact* magazine. The volume contains many of Williams' most anthologized poems, including "The Red Wheelbarrow," "To Elsie," and the poem now often known as "Spring and All."

The piece is also very commonly referred to by its first line, "By the road to the contagious hospital." The line is important as it not only sets the context for the poem but it also qualifies all of the natural imagery that is to follow. (It also qualifies the setting of the twenty-eight vignettes that follow in the full sequence of poems). The "contagious hospital" is the more conspicuous of only two images of the man-made in the poem; however, because it is first, and is the first participial phrase, thereby qualifying all the lines that follow, it effectively brackets the imagery of the poem in a space of contagion and, by extension, failure and death. In the 1920s, contagious hospitals served as places of quarantine where patients with contagious diseases such as polio or tuberculosis were sent for treatment. It was widely thought that if a person wound up there, he or she would not return.

Despite this qualifying opening, the poem is not about death. The road is the other man-made image in the poem. Roads allow for travel, arrival and departure, and so the road serves as a connection to other fates. But, as the first line states, it is a road *to* the hospital, and so presumably comes to an end where patients enter. Hence, while the road can function to bring people and to send them on, the poem calls our attention to only one purpose of the road.

Throughout the remainder of the first stanza, the participial phrases continue to pile upon one another, and on into the following couplet, with no active verb to reveal any present action. Verbs are used only in adverbial positions. As a result, the surroundings in the poem have heightened significance. Williams' enjambments add to their importance. The second line's "surge of the blue" has the potential for lyric and imaginative possibility at the end of the line. Even after it is clear in the next line that the "mottled clouds" are blue, the result is unexpected, given how often clouds are described as white or grey. The use of the word "mottled," in such proximity to "contagious," connotes disease, making the sky almost pestilential.

After two lines that seem to pause at their ends, the third and fourth lines end on "the," forcing readers quickly to the next line. The poem therefore creates a feeling of slight unease, since the poet is employing a number of strategies in how he chooses to treat the end of his lines. Some draw us on; others play on the pause for effect. The overall result is that the first two stanzas mimic the flitting attentions of an eye discovering the landscape around it. Several stanzas later, encountering the line "One by one objects are defined—," it becomes clear that there must be *some* process of seeing, whether it is a perspective of a person working itself out, or if it is simply the sunrise bringing gradually more light and rendering the surroundings increasingly clear.

The early surroundings are also described with a series of charged words. The wind, from the northeast, is "cold;" in northern New Jersey, Williams' home and the setting for the vast majority of his work, a cold northeast wind is often foreboding of worse weather to follow. To northeastern readers at least, the very thought would be grim. "Beyond, the/ waste" again reinforces the desolation and sickness, and even its contagious spread to all that surrounds the hospital. Finally, the stanza ends with "dried weeds, standing and fallen" and thus at different stages of decay or bearing. As the eye takes in the entire landscape and scene, the next couplet becomes even less particular than when it observes the variety of stances in the weeds. The water is in patches, the trees are simply tall. Williams knew his region, and thus its flora and fauna, often invoking the correct names, cultures, and legends of many plants in other poems. To have not done so here is an important decision on his part. He has effectively lumped the landscape into a single image of decay in these early stanzas.

Many critics have pointed out that at the beginning of the third stanza, it is almost as if the poem starts again. The previous couplet's homogenous descriptions give way to much description: "the reddish/ purplish, forked, upstanding, twiggy/ stuff of bushes and small trees" is a far cry from the waste of brown in previous lines. The colors are vigorous, and the red and purple hues are of hardy stems prepared for new growth. The "dead, brown leaves under them/ leafless vines" are what has been cast away to prepare for what is next: "Lifeless in appearance, sluggish / dazed spring approaches—" Spring is here characterized in unusual terms, sluggish, dazed, as though it has itself only just come to life after long slumber, or as a new creature to the world, just born. The dash that ends the stanza, just as the one that ends the previous stanza, pushes us on to what's to come. It is yet another example of Williams' varied treatment of his line breaks.

The pronoun of the following stanza is the first point where the poem makes reference to a subject about which it is ostensibly concerned. "They" could be a number of things, and critics have made guesses as to what "they" might be: people, plants, or ideas. A literal reading strongly suggests that "they" are the plants. That reading is confounded a bit by the remainder of the line: "They enter the new world naked" implies that there is a clothed state. That the world is new implies, again, birth. The second line of the stanza uses enjambment again in such a way as to draw our attention to the "uncertainty of all." Cold is repeated twice in this stanza, underscoring the violence of birth and all its uncertainties, and further developing the dichotomy that is the poem's purpose: that within the death of contagion and waste, there is still this great birth and terrible violence of newness. That the wind at the end of the fifth stanza is "familiar" suggests again that the subject of this poem is flora. However, the word familiar here possesses overtones beyond the literal definition, and in the context of birth, may hint at something familiar at the instinctive level, at least from the perspective of the narration.

In the couplets that follow, the sixth and seventh stanzas of the poem, respectively, the narrator of the poem becomes far more particular about the surroundings than in the early stanzas. Here grass is referred to specifically, as is "wildcarrot leaf," complete with the lyrical description of it. The couplet stands alone, gathering its power from the preceding setting and the drama of "Now," which acts verbally to push the details to the very present. The "now" repeats again in the final stanza, but only after another couplet wherein the poem tells that the details of the scene are emerging and sharpening, just as one focuses vision or becomes aware of surroundings. As stated above, it is as though dawn is bringing particularities into relief. Here, too, Williams is specific, but not in the same manner as in the previous couplet. He is not naming particular plants; rather, the eye of the poem has gone from noticing clumps of trees and fields to noticing a singular "outline of leaf," thereby seeing the singular drama and interest in what is otherwise a wasting landscape.

That sight changes the character of the entire situation. In the final stanza, the poem now characterizes the birth or rebirth as an entrance of "stark dignity." Taken together, all the imagery and realization become "the profound change," causing the newcomers to "grip down and begin to awaken." The grammar here is still as challenging and inconclusive as in the beginning stanzas, but it is no longer a series of qualifications. Instead, the poem has become a series of declarations and revisions by the narrator. The poem uses both lyric technique and a series of images adorned only with charged modifiers to complicate the vision of the landscape as one of birth amid nearly overwhelming death and contagion.

"Spring and All"

DAVID WALKER ON THE POEM'S JUXTAPOSITION
OF NARRATIVE AND IMAGE

[David Walker is Department Chair and Professor of English at Oberlin College. He is the author of *The Transparent Lyric* and many articles about modern and contemporary literature. He is co-editor of *FIELD: Contemporary Poetry and Poetics* and of Oberlin College Press He also edited *A FIELD Guide to Contemporary Poetry and Poetics* and *Poets Reading: The FIELD Symposia.* In his exploration of the modern lyric, Walker, in this excerpt, looks at how the poem juxtaposes two different modes of lyric expression without compromising either, reflecting the larger and lifelong struggle in Williams' poetics between poetry and prose.]

In some of his poems of the 1920s, Williams succeeds in further submerging the dramatic role of the speaker, avoiding assertive statements of judgment or insight, while at the same time building on structures of tension or dialectical process in order to avoid the static quality he believed by this time to be the failure of imagism. The subject of *Spring and All* (1923) is the dynamic energy of the imagination, and the structure of the volume as a whole, darting erratically between poetry and prose, serves to transfer that energy to the reading experience. Individual poems also formally evoke the same kind of activity. One of the most familiar, "By the road to the contagious hospital" (*CEP*, 241–42), may be seen as transitional between the dramatic lyric and the transparent lyric. Its structure reflects the dynamic tension between a static, almost photographic description of the landscape and an intuition of the organic energies of growth inherent in the landscape—which is in turn mimetic of the conflict in the volume between winter and spring, or the conflict in Williams' poetics between prose and poetry. The beginning of the poem, aside from the ubiquitous circumstances of selection and arrangement, is almost entirely free of evidence of Williams' "presence" as a poet:

By the road to the contagious hospital
under the surge of the blue
mottled clouds driven from the
northeast—a cold wind. Beyond, the
waste of broad, muddy fields
brown with dried weeds, standing and fallen

patches of standing water
the scattering of tall trees

All along the road the reddish
purplish, forked, upstanding, twiggy
stuff of bushes and small trees
with dead, brown leaves under them
leafless vines—

We recognize, of course, Williams' careful use of sound, lineation, and repetition ("standing . . . standing . . . upstanding") to control the way we apprehend this world; but the world itself we seem to experience directly, through its own colors, textures, and shapes, rather than through any extravagantly subjective metaphors the poet might impose on it. That the blue clouds "surge" instead of "rush" or "billow," and that the muddy fields compose a "waste," does imply a measure of judgment, but certainly the predominant impression is of impersonal observation. As the focus shifts from present circumstances to immanence and possibility, though, the poem moves through sympathetic projection into the landscape:

Lifeless in appearance, sluggish
dazed spring approaches—

They enter the new world naked,
cold, uncertain of all
save that they enter. All about them
the cold, familiar wind—

As the new, vital organisms are personified, the central consciousness of the poem itself comes into view, reflecting, in Stevens' terms, not a mind of winter but the tendency to see natural forms in human terms. In the final stanzas, the two modes of the poem alternate, moving from the knowing anticipation of "Now the grass, tomorrow / the stiff curl of wildcarrot leaf" to the nearly scientific precision of "One by one objects are defined— / It quickens: clarity, outline of leaf," and then back to humanized description:

But now the stark dignity of
entrance—Still, the profound change
has come upon them: rooted, they
grip down and begin to awaken

Roy Harvey Pearce says of the poem, "A perception of a series of
objects is made to blend into a thought ('It quickens:'), so that it *is*
the thought." I believe rather that the two kinds of apprehension are
juxtaposed but *not* blended, and that the tension between them is a
crucial aspect of the reading experience.

—David Walker, *The Transparent Lyric: Reading and Meaning in the
Poetry of Stevens and Williams* (Princeton: Princeton University
Press, 1984): pp. 140-142.

AUDREY RODGERS ON WILLIAM'S USE OF DEMETER/KORE MYTH

[Audrey Rodgers is retired as Professor of English at the
Pennsylvania State University. Her other books include *The
Universal Drum: Dance Imagery in the Poetry of Eliot,
Crane, Roethke, and Williams* and *Denise Levertov: The
Poetry of Engagement.* In the excerpt, Rodgers discusses the
evolution of Williams' themes of violation and rebirth as
manifest in his female characters, and shows how the
themes are brought together in "Spring and All."]

. . . [I]t is in *Spring and All* that the poet brings together the themes
of violation and the redemptive return of spring, first in "To Elsie"
and then in "Spring and All". That "the pure products of America go
crazy" is borne out in the deflowering of Elsie and her transformation into a young slattern. The poem is a masterpiece of Williams'
indictment of the contemporary world. It traces the inevitable dese-
cration of innocence in the shape of the young Elsie, who comes to
the city, falls prey to its shoddy temptations, and finally is violated
by a society that experiences little remorse or responsibility. Yet,
Williams notes, we all bear the burden, and the debasement of Elsie
debases us all. "To Elsie" is a sobering comment upon the innocent
victims of an industrialized society that has lost its direction, its
humanity, its conscience—save for vague murmurings of a more
transcendent, regenerative way of life:

> some Elsie—
> voluptuous water
> expressing with broken
>
> brain the truth about us—

In "Spring and All" Williams articulates the theme that out of such death and decay, "by the road to the contagious hospital," it is possible for spring to return, and the poet traces the almost invisible signs of rebirth—admittedly an experience of incalculable mystery, as the ". . . reddish/ purplish, forked, upstanding, twiggy/ stuff of bushes and small trees/ with dead, brown leaves under them . . ." yield up new life:

> Lifeless in appearance, sluggish
> dazed spring approaches—
>
> They enter the new world naked,
> cold, uncertain of all
> save that they enter.

—Audrey Rodgers, *Virgin and Whore: The Image of Women in the Poetry of William Carlos Williams* (Jefferson: McFarland & Company, Inc., 1987): pp. 35-36.

PETER SCHMIDT ON THE BIBLICAL ALLUSIONS IN THE POEM

[Peter Schmidt is Professor of English at Swarthmore College and is the author of *The Heart of the Story: Eudora Welty's Short Fiction* and *William Carlos Williams, The Arts, and Literary Traditions*, and co-editor of *Postcolonial Theory and the United States: Race, Ethnicity, and Literature*. The excerpt discusses the poem's echoes of Genesis in the context of Schmidt's larger handling of the differences between Williams' pastoral and urban poems.]

When the whole of Williams' urban and rural pastoral lyrics are compared, essential differences emerge. Williams' urban poems tend to consider social issues and the correct relation of artifice and nature. His nature lyrics, on the other hand, ground these humanistic issues in a larger, inhuman context; while they may celebrate nature's bounty, and even compare it with what man can produce, they most often portray what the poem "Spring and All" (1923) calls the "stark dignity" of life's entrance or exit, not its healthy (or decadent) middle. Like "Chicory and Daisies," these lyrics are concerned with the creation and destruction of a world. This too is a traditional topic of pastoral poetry—perhaps its most ambitious one.

Williams' most famous treatment of such a birth, of course, is the title poem of *Spring and All* (Poem I). Drawing together most of the features of Williams' other Precisionist pastoral lyrics—including their merging of still life and landscape, their use of personification, and their innovative celebration of both man-made and natural objects—"Spring and All" also reminds us of the Adamic or Messianic impulse within traditional pastoral poetry and alludes modestly but very explicitly to its sources in Genesis and the Messianic Fourth Eclogue of Vergil.

When "Spring and All" begins, Williams is driving "on the road to the contagious hospital" where victims of contagious diseases are treated (*CP1*, 183). From his car window, he has difficulty seeing outline or order in the landscape: *mottled, patches, waste,* and *scattering* are some of the words he uses. His problems culminate in the third stanza, where inexact adjectives, often afflicted with the suffixes *ish* or *y,* glut an entire line before a noun can be found. And even then the noun is imprecise:

> All along the road the reddish
> purplish, forked, upstanding, twiggy
> stuff . . .
> (*CP1*, 183)

Like the diseases in the hospital Williams is approaching, imprecision is a debilitating contagion of the mind.

As "one by one objects are defined" by spring, however, Williams' language is also reborn, and he can foresee the appearance of the wildcarrot, the only named species in the poem. His battle to see and to name has a "stark dignity" equal to spring's battle with winter, or a chicory's battle to create light from darkness. Like the plants, the poet's mind must "grip down," struggling to wrest a name from anonymity. The right name is a strong root; new poetry, and a new world, will grow from it as invincibly as the wildcarrot leaf uncurls. But the hidden *source* of names and new plants remains mysterious, identified only through an impersonal pronoun ("it quickens") (*CP1*, 183). As Thomas Whitaker has pointed out, the nouns and pronouns of the last stanzas of the poem are simultaneously precise and vague. The "all" created by nature may be named and enumerated, but "spring," the creative source itself, remains unknowable.

Like many pastoral lyrics, "Spring and All" alludes to an Eden or a Golden Age, the loss of it, and its eventual return. In the Bible, of course, such an event signifies the end of history, whereas in Vergil and other classical writers it inaugurates yet another historical cycle. Williams' poem well represents romanticism's distinctive revision of this archetypal plot. The large historical cycles between Iron and Golden Ages, or Old Adam and New Messiah, are internalized and speeded up: the rebirth experienced in "Spring and All," like spring itself, is continually lost, found, and lost again. Williams' poem ends poised on the verge of awakening, looking backward toward winter yet foreseeing spring:

> Now the grass, tomorrow
> the stiff curl of wildcarrot leaf
>
> One by one objects are defined
> It quickens: clarity, outline of leaf
>
> But now the stark dignity of
> entrance—Still, the profound change
> has come upon them: rooted, they
> grip down and begin to awaken
> (*CP1*, 183)

—Peter Schmidt, *William Carlos Williams, The Arts, and Literary Traditions* (Baton Rouge: Louisiana State University Press, 1988): pp. 41-43.

BARRY AHEARN ON METAMORPHOSIS IN THE POEM

[Barry Ahearn is Professor of English at Tulane University. He is the author of *William Carlos Williams and Alterity* and *Zukofsky's "A": An Introduction.* Ahearn connects the metamorphosis of spring in the poem with the reinvention of language for which Williams struggles in the complete sequence of *Spring and All*.]

Of course the most famous celebration of seasonal change we find in Williams's work, and the one with which we will close this section of our examination of metamorphosis, is the first poem of *Spring and All*. The visual metamorphosis in "Spring and All" involves the transformation of a "waste of broad, muddy fields" (1.5) into a landscape rich with growing vegetation. The natural change has significance for *Spring and All* only as a metaphor to which other changes are allied, such as the revitalization of language. Williams begins his poem with a crowd of prepositional phrases long before the appearance of an active verb. Whitman used the same device in some of his major poems; prepositional phrases dominated the first sentence of "Out of the Cradle Endlessly Rocking." That sentence continues for nineteen lines before reaching the subject ("I," l. 20) and predicate ("sing," l. 22). Commentators on Whitman have rightly compared that first sentence to an operatic overture, but it also creates a landscape in which the young Whitman has a relatively minor role in comparison with his surroundings. Since prepositions do describe relations between objects, any poem commencing with a large number of them will be furnished with a complex landscape. We find six prepositions in the first four lines of "Spring and All," which makes the beginning sufficiently busy. But since he does not include himself in the scene, Williams offers a landscape without focus. The language of the first eight lines of "Spring and All" expresses a random search that leads nowhere. In line 9 the poem starts over, but with a difference. Now it has a focus: "the reddish / purplish, forked, upstanding, twiggy / stuff of bushes and small trees' (Ll. 9–11). These are the first signs of life in the spring. The linguistic counterpart in the poem is the appearance of the four unusual words that comprise line 10. These words should be approached with caution. We must distinguish between two ways of meaning: dictionary definitions of particular words and (as Williams remarks in his essay on Marianne Moore) the way in which the words pertain to other words in the field of the poem. The words of line 10 all have assignable meanings, but we must also recognize that they are seldom encountered in everyday discourse. The rarity of the words in line 10, therefore, lends it a special distinction. That line stands out in the poem: so do the plants quickening with life in the dead landscape.

As Williams goes on to enliven the linguistic dimension of the poem, he finally achieves an active verb in line 15: "dazed spring approaches –." The high proportion of active verbs in the poem's second half further suggests the potency of nature's burgeoning life. Another parallel to the quickening of life in a wasteland appears in the cinematic dimension of the poem. Just before "Spring and All," Williams domments on the Elgin Marbles:

> In that huge and microscopic career of time, as it were a wild horse racing in an illimitable pampa under the stars, describing immense and microscopic circles with his hoofs on the solid turf, running without a stop for the millionth part of a second until he is aged and worn to a heap of skin, bones and ragged hoofs—In that majestic progress of life, that gives the exact impression of Phidias' frieze, the men and beasts of which, though they seem of the rigidity of marble are not so but move, with blinding rapidity, though we do not have the time to notice it, their legs advancing a millionth part of an inch every fifty thousand years—In that progress of life which seems stillness itself in the mass of its movements—at last SPRING is approaching. (*CPI*, 182)

The difference between this account of Attic sculptures and that of Keats in his "Ode on a Grecian Urn" (Williams surely has in mind Keats's imphasis on the eternal stasis of the figure in the urn) lies in the change from a static, sculptural, Idealist point of view, which Williams associates with an outmoded art, to a dynamic, cinematic, quotidian art, which he champions. To put the distinction succinctly, we might call it the difference between the sculptural and the cinematic.

Later in the poem, Williams links the rebirth of the year with the cinema in lines 20 through 23: "Now the grass, tomorrow / the stiff curl of wildcarrot leaf / / One by one objects are defined—/ It quickens: clarity, otuline of leaf." This portion of the poem offers a prospective view of the next stage of vegetable growth, at a quicker tempo than actual growth. We have the verbal equivalent of the cinematic nature studies in which flowers bloom in moments rather than in hours. The scene, though sketchy in those four lines, rapidly grows. Williams recognized that the technique of the motion picture, with its ability to compress time, was well suited for depicting metamorphosis.

—Barry Ahearn, *William Carlos Williams and Alterity: The Early Poetry* (New York: Cambridge University Press, 1994): pp. 114-116.

PETER HALTER ON THE POEM'S FORM AND THE MIND'S ARRANGEMENT OF DETAIL

[Peter Halter is Professor of American Literature at the University of Laussanne. His other books include *Katherine Mansfield und die Kurzgeschichte, William Shakespeare: Measure for Measure,* and *The Revolution in the Visual Arts and the Poetry of William Carlos Williams.* In this selection from a chapter describing formal matters occurring in the visual arts and in Williams' poems, Halter discusses the contrasting formal aspects of "Spring and All" and "The Red Wheelbarrow" to argue that patterned and non-patterned forms in Williams do not automatically signify coherence or defeat when viewing a chaotic reality.]

. . . Sayre distills "two types of poems" which are based upon "competing aesthetic assumptions":

On the one hand, [Williams] would have it that the mind represents itself by the abstract designs it discovers and creates, by the order it imposes on reality. On the other hand, whenever his poems are most clearly about the mind, they tend to be disorderly. In one kind of poem the imagination is defined as the place from which form and order spring; in the other, especially in contrast to the first, the imagination seems to be disorder's natural home. (p. 74)

Many of the "disorderly" or loose poems, according to Sayre, reflect "the lack of a bridge between the chaotic world and the ordering mind," and it is this "divorce of the writing from the vision" that "seems to justify the lack of form" (p. 73).

Now it seems to me that Sayre's distinction between the two basic types of poem is highly useful but does not do justice to the second form. It is problematic, above all, to classify the patterned variant as the one that achieves a formal order and clarity while the other, looser form fails to do so and is therefore a document of Williams's frustration or despair. One argument against such a division consists in the fact that many of Williams's loose poems—among them "The Rose," "Spring and All," "Crimson Cyclamen," "A Marriage Ritual," and "Rain"—are predominantly affirmative, while a number of poems written in the stanzaic form (particularly among those written in the 1930s and the 1940s, such as "A Portrait of the Times," "You Have Pissed Your Life," "A Bastard Peace," "These") are written in a dark or pessimistic mood.

However, one may well take one's cue from Sayre's distinction without subscribing to his conclusion that the patterned form is a sign of success while the "disorderly" form denotes a declaration of defeat before a chaotic present that defies being transformed in the work of art by the ordering mind. The loose poems are indeed more concerned with the ordering mind, while the patterned poems predominantly explore the tension between the recalcitrant object-world and the "design" or order imposed on it. The patterned form often exploits the tension between object-world and work of art; the loose form on the other hand explores the tension between self and other, with the mind incessantly engaged—sometimes successfully and sometimes not—in bringing about order.

The first, patterned kind, in other words, is more concerned with the tension between the concrete and the abstract, the mimetic and nonmimetic, while the second makes of the poem an embodiment of the act of discovery or exploration. It consists essentially of the *process* of exploration, of the self entering the (new) world naked. Each of these poems enacts a new approach, since each is about a new creation of order, at least the attempt to bring it about.

The difference between the two forms emerges very clearly when we compare "The Red Wheelbarrow" with an equally exemplary poem of the second kind, "Spring and All" (*CP1*, 183). In both poems, for instance, Williams exploits the tension between lineation and syntax, in the sense that line unit and sense unit are often not identical. This means that in both poems, as we have seen, words are at one and the same time referential and self-referential; the poem becomes a network of linguistic tensions based on dissonance and clash rather than on the harmony resulting from an identity of sense unit and line unit. One of the best descriptions of this effect is in J. Hillis Miller's *Poets of Reality*:

> Conjunctions, prepositions, adjectives, when they come at the end of a line, assume an expressive energy as arrows of force reaching toward the other words: "of red and→." Going for the moment toward the void, they go all the more strongly, as a man in isolation reaches out in longing toward other men and women. Into the white space surrounding the word go a multitude of lines of force, charging that space with the almost tangible presence of the various words which might come to complete the central world and appease its tension. (p. 300)

The effects of enjambments as described here can be observed in both the loose and the patterned poems. However, enjambments can also have different effects in the two forms, and this difference can tell us more about the constitutive traits of each of them. Thus in "The Red Wheelbarrow," "wheel / barrow" and "rain / water" cut the compounds into their constituents, which makes us aware of the fact "that they are phenomenological constituents as well," as John Hollander put it: "The wheel plus the barrow equals the wheelbarrow, and in the freshness of light after the rain . . . things seem to lose their compounded properties." Enjambment here is used as a means of defamiliarization, which gives us back something of Ruskin's "innocence of the eye" and prevents us from seeing, as Valéry would have said, with the dictionary instead of the eyes.

On the other hand, a line break such as the following from the opening lines of "Spring and All" has, at least partly, a different effect:

> under the surge of the blue
> mottled clouds . . .

"Blue" is a noun when we take the line as a unit in itself, but it becomes an adjective the moment we reach the next line. The eye of the viewer exploring a landscape—not unlike that of a viewer confronted with the ambiguous elements in a Cubist canvas—is engaged in a process of disambiguation: The poet or persona, surrounded by a somewhat chaotic landscape, sees, at first more or less disorientedly, a multitude of details and gradually sorts them out until the whole scenery is "defined," in a process that reenacts the resurgence of life in early spring. The form of the poem, in other words, iconically embodies the gradual emergence of form in, and from, a landscape which at the beginning of the poem is still "a waste of broad, muddy fields / brown with dried weeds, standing and fallen," but which moves step by step toward a greater "clarity, outline of form." The shift from "blue" as noun to adjective is thus part of this iconic enactment of form being born and stands for one of the many moments of (re)orientation. From the spots of blue in the sky the eye is pulled to the "mottled clouds" so that "blue," at first a noun, becomes a metonymically displaced adjective—instead of a blue sky with mottled clouds we get a sky with "blue / mottled Clouds." This displacement conveys the feeling of nervous shifts from one detail to another, as well as the sense of a slight disorientation, which is reinforced by the enjambments of the next two lines:

> . . . the blue
> mottled clouds driven from the
>
> northeast—a cold wind. Beyond
> the waste . . .

Both of these run-on lines leave the reader hung up for a moment with the deictic "the" at the end, with a definite article that is severed from the noun belonging to it. The first enjambment can be read as a short hesitation before relating the direction of the wind to the cardinal points, while the second enjambment contains, as it were, the fraction of a second that the mind sometimes needs before it can name what has just caught the eye.

The entire poem is characterized by these nervous shifts. All is process here, and all is motion. Almost all the sentences are either fragmentary or elliptical, and the poem consists of incessant new beginnings and reorientations. One sentence overlaps another, or one sentence fragment stops where the next begins. Adverbials such as "now," "tomorrow," "But now," "one by one" indicate temporal jumps and modifications in which the mind is continuously pulled back and forth between a (conceived) temporal or seasonal progression and a (perceived) immediate present, a present, however, which is in itself embodiment of continuous change.

—Peter Halter, *The Revolution in the Visual Arts and the Poetry of William Carlos Williams* (New York: Cambridge University Press, 1994): pp. 189-91.

BRUCE COMENS ON THE POEM'S PLACE IN WILLIAMS'
APOCALYPTIC VISION

[Bruce Comens is a writer and critic who teaches at Temple University. He earned his Ph.D. at SUNY–Buffalo, and is the author of *Apocalypse and After: Modern Strategy and Postmodern Tactics in Pound, Williams, and Zukofsky*. This excerpt outlines how the poem lies at an important crux in Williams' developing vision of the need for apocalypse and rebirth, and that the poem as a result works as an overture for work to come.]

It is at this climactic moment, the moment of rebirth, that Williams presents the book's first poem, "By the road to the contagious hospital," also known as "Spring and All." Poetry, seemingly, will provide the answer, the fulfillment of Williams'—and the reader's—desire to achieve contact. This is precisely the claim Miller makes for Williams' art: where the prose of *Spring and All* remains caught within inescapable "conceptual circles," in his poetic practice "Williams at last takes possession of the presence of the present, of that eternal moment in which we alone live. It is a present, however, that is not perceptual but linguistic, a present not present except in words" (*Linguistic Moment,* 381). And Miller in fact cites a few stanzas of "By the road" as evidence of what he rather vaguely calls the "curious immediacy" Williams achieves "in or between the words of his poems" (387, 384). Indeed, both "By the road" and the immediately following poem, "Pink confused with white," insist on their own presence by enacting a disruption of habit in its own way as violent as the previous apocalypse. To the reader who, like a driver on a road, has been comfortably skimming along lines of prose, not attending to what is there because intent on getting elsewhere, the first lines must come as something of a shock:

> By the road to the contagious hospital
> under the surge of the blue
> mottled clouds driven from the
> northeast—a cold wind. Beyond, the
> waste of broad, muddy fields
> brown with dried weeds, standing and fallen
> (*I*, 95)

The first line ends with a comfortable (almost "natural") break at the end of a phrase. The second line first delays the expected subject (we must read slightly more attentively to retain control) and then ends abruptly and confusingly—if we assume the line coincides with the phrasal unit and take "blue" as a noun, presumably synecdochic for "sky," we are left with the expressive but nearly nonsensical "surge of the sky." Instead, we plunge on, assuming "blue" to be an adjective, an assumption that is quickly confirmed. A line ending with an adjective, if unusual, is still explicable (done for emphasis), so the disruption remains minor. It is, though, naggingly persistent: blue clouds are not what realistic literature usually gives us. We can, of course, refer to the poem's miming of the author's experience: he notices the "surge" while not looking directly, looks and sees "blue," and then, before the mind can supply "sky" (for he is still searching for the "surge"), sees the mottling and identifies the clouds as the source of the surge. But that reading could only come later; it requires time, a leisure that the poem refuses to provide. If our attention is now stimulated by these unexpected breaks, our curiosity mildly aroused, the third line, still delaying the subject and ending with "the," engages us in an active struggle to maintain control, to make sense, compelling our attention onward to line four. In that line, interestingly, "northeast" presents a significant shift from perceptual particulars to a conceptual response—no doubt the difficult line break records this sudden distancing. But "northeast" remains a particular, and the line goes on to provide only the banality of "a cold wind" as climax, the cause of disruption and therefore focus of attention. And we still do not have a sentence. The lack of a verb, while not interfering with the sense of these lines, increases the feeling of being thrown in among perceptual particulars, refusing to allow us the comfort and distance afforded by a "complete thought." There is, to be sure, a certain feeling of closure, of completion at this point. Counteracting this effect, however, "Beyond, the" combines semantic and syntactic forces to push us onward even more forcefully than what has preceded. Perception will not now linger. Once broken out of convention, once freed of habit, it pushes on immediately, or "instanter," as Charles Olson has it, leaving reason off balance and therefore unable to assemble, to summarize—and so return to conventional patterns of inattention (*Human Universe,* 53).

The poem continues to immerse the reader in accumulating particulars for the next two stanzas, providing no verb and thus no "complete thought." Throughout, the isolation of words and the disruption of syntax produce a sense of immediacy and force the reader to confront the presence of the poem. But then, precisely halfway through the poem, a significant shift occurs, as Williams supplies one verb, one "complete thought," after another. Here is the last half of the poem:

> Lifeless in appearance, sluggish
> dazed spring approaches—
>
> They enter the new world naked,
> cold, uncertain of all
> save that they enter. All about them
> the cold, familiar wind—
>
> Now the grass, tomorrow
> the stiff curl of wildcarrot leaf
>
> One by one objects are defined—
> It quickens: clarity, outline of leaf
>
> But now the stark dignity of
> entrance—Still, the profound change
> has come upon them: rooted, they
> grip down and begin to awake
> (*I,* 95–96)

Clearly, this poem begins to build anew: just as the explosive activity of birth is followed by more settled growth, so the poem returns to the stable forms requisite to conceptual understanding, to strategic control. Note, too, the return of narrative order and predictive ability in "Now the grass, tomorrow the stiff curl," and the way objects settle into clear definitions and outlines—structures that return the observer to distanced objectivity.

Struggling against this return, Williams in the final stanza tries to insist again on the rebirth itself, but the moment can be neither prolonged nor retrieved. A "profound change" may have occurred, but the intensity of that moment cannot be sustained; Miller's "presence of the present" may be entered, but it cannot be possessed. The reversion to expected syntax and semantics, then, mimes Williams' own distance while also distancing the reader—words begin to lose their newly acquired immediacy as we in effect return to the ossifications of habit. And so the poem ends, enacting precisely the same dilemma as the preceding prose, and in language closer to prose than it at first had used. The poetry of *Spring and All* can no more sustain immediacy, can no more offer a solution, than the prose.

—Bruce Comens, *Apocalypse and After: Modern Strategy and Postmodern Tactics in Pound, Williams, and Zukofsky* (Tuscaloosa: University of Alabama Press, 1995): pp. 98-100

JOHN LOWNEY ON THE POEM'S PLACE IN WILLIAM'S POETICS OF DISSENT

[John Lowney is Assistant Professor of English at St. John's University. He is the author of *The American Avant-Garde Tradition: William Carlos Williams, Postmodern Poetry, and the Politics of Cultural Memory* as well as a number of critical articles. Lowney contends that "William's poetics of dissent" (his term) is manifest in the book *Spring and All*, wherein the poems question a number of polarities in American culture. Lowney points out that the "title poem," if you will, contains the most compelling examples of the sorts of ideas Williams goes on to question: the polarity of poetry and prose, rich and poor, birth and death, etc.]

The famous opening poem of *Spring and All*, later titled "Spring and All," epitomizes the physician's vision as poet's vision, while exemplifying the themes and techniques Williams explores throughout the book. The opening line of "Spring and All," "By the road to the contagious hospital" (*CP1*, 183), places the poem in a medical context. The adjective *contagious* suggests that the hospital is itself contagious, that it does not contain disease, that sickness is an ever-present state in this bleak landscape. The entire book, as well as this poem itself, can be seen as Williams's response to Eliot's depiction of the modern world as a wasteland. But it should also be seen as Williams's response to the wasteland world of poverty and disease he knew as a doctor. "Williams's rendering of his wasteland of clouds, cold, mud, and dead plants gives it a stark beauty, however. The "purplish, forked, upstanding, twiggy / stuff of bushes and small trees" (*CP1*, 183) stands not as thematic background but as something worth examining in itself. The poem's lineation compels us to notice the singularities and connections of these roadside images. There is no punctuation at the ends of lines, and the syntactic sense often precludes an expected end stop. For example, in the lines "under the surge of the blue / mottled clouds driven from the northeast" (*CP1*, 183), "blue" and "mottled" are separated by the line break, yet they are semantically fused. The eye jumps from what is normally an adjective, "blue," to the next line to find the noun, "clouds," but the line break suggests that "the blue" is itself an entity. The lineation produces the effect of a windy spring sky, the "blue mottled clouds" changing so rapidly that we must pay close attention to distinguish "blue" from "clouds." Similarly, the lines "purplish, forked, upstanding, twiggy / stuff of bushes and small trees" (*CP1*, 183) achieve this sense of dynamic process. These adjectives are separated by commas, and although they all modify "stuff," they evoke individual plants before jumping from "twiggy" to "stuff of bushes and small trees." The effect is one of constant shifts in perspective, from the clouds to the fields to patterns of landscape to details of the roadside growth—all portrayed without grammatical connectives. This process of vision and revision resembles the doctor's openness to his patients' attempts to articulate their symptoms. Like the patient, the landscape is approached and examined "naked, just as it was, without a lie, telling itself . . . in its own terms" (*A*, 357).

Williams's thematic retort to Eliot's more pessimistic vision occurs later in the poem; when in Williams's landscape spring arrives, life is renewed:

> They enter the new world naked
> cold, uncertain of all

save that they enter. All about them
the cold, familiar wind
(*CP1*, 183)

"They," following the approach of "sluggish dazed spring," evokes the shoots growing from the earth, but the syntax leaves the referent of "they" ambivalent, suggesting a more general concept of birth, physical rebirth that is spiritual in the sense of absolute faith in rebirth, "uncertain of all / save that they enter." The wind is "familiar," not shocking, to the newborn simply because there are no preconceptions in plant life, or in newborn life in general: the newborn adapt to environmental conditions that become immediately "familiar" because there is no sense of otherness. The late winter wasteland will give birth to spring whether we interpret it or not; the child will struggle to survive whether it is cared for or not.

The conclusion of "Spring and All" reiterates Williams's physician's vision of examining the world empirically, rather than symbolically: "One by one, objects are defined— / It quickens: clarity, outline of leaf" (*CP1*, 183). These lines epitomize Williams's rejection of "crude symbolism" in *Spring and All*: "The word must be put down for itself, not as a symbol of nature but a part, cognizant of the whole—aware—civilized" (*CP1*, 189). The "clarity, outline of leaf" represents not only the "leaf" of spring growth but the page as "outline of leaf" as well, the frame that directs our attention to the "clarity" of vision the words evoke. Hugh Kenner incisively summarizes Williams's poetic vision in terms that are also applicable to the doctor's vision: "This ability to move close to quite simple words, both hearing them as spoken—not quite the same thing as hearing their sounds—and seeing them interact on a typewritten page, gives Williams the sense of constant discovery. . . . 'No ideas but in things' meant that the energy moving from word to word would be like that of the eye moving from thing to thing, and not like that of the predicating faculty with its opinions." The closing imagery of "Spring and All" articulates the doctor's and the poet's "sense of constant discovery" in the figure of birth as rebirth. The newborn are "rooted," as they "grip down" through their roots and "begin to awaken." From the decay of winter arises the rebirth of spring growth; from the poverty of northern New Jersey arises the will to survive. Although death and decay are ever-present, the promise of new life and rebirth never disappears. There are no sentimental notions about spring here, only a belief in the indomitable will to be born, to survive.

The figure of birth that closes "Spring and All" typifies Williams's insistence throughout *Spring and All* for new forms and new language to return poetry to everyday life. The book begins with a characteristically avant-garde gesture, an overtly antagonistic challenge to its readers: "If anything of moment results—so much the better. And so much the more likely will it be that no one will want to see it" (*CP1*, 177). Not only a "sour grapes" reflection on critical reactions to Williams's previous books, this introductory statement redefines the colloquialism "anything of moment" into an epistemological, ethical, aesthetic imperative to counteract the "constant barrier between the reader and his consciousness of immediate contact with the world" (ibid.). Williams's project in *Spring and All* entails not so much establishing this "contact" as exposing and subverting poetic strategies that divert the imagination from any "articulation" of its immediate world. This simultaneously destructive and creative project requires a productive reader whom Williams defines in dialogic, intersubjective terms: "Whenever I say, 'I,' I mean also, 'you'" (*CP1*, 178). Only writing that produces such an author/reader relationship can engage the reader's imagination.

—John Lowney, *The American Avant-Garde Tradition: William Carlos Williams, Postmodern Poetry, and the Politics of Cultural Memory* (Lewisburg: Bucknell University Press, 1997): pp. 62-64.

CRITICAL ANALYSIS OF

"The Yachts"

"The Yachts" first appeared in *The New Republic*, and was included in 1935's *An Early Martyr and Other Poems,* a collection which featured poems predominantly concerned with working class stories and characters, and which overall was less experimental than Williams' earlier collections. In it, one can see glimmers of the characters that will come to populate the epic *Paterson.*

"The Yachts," however, has its sources far from Paterson, New Jersey, in the America's Cup races Williams remembered watching in Rhode Island years before he wrote the poem. The poem begins with the title, and moves into a formal opening that, for only the first two stanzas, is in *terza rima*. When the poem moves away from the governing rhyme scheme that characterizes the form, it still persists in three-line stanzas, a formality that is congruent with the image: the boats and their geometry, the enclosure, the structure of a race, and the water as a dividing line between what is above and below.

The first line describes the protected bay wherein the yachts race. The narrator reiterates later that the area is protected. The choices of words he uses to characterize the protection—shielding, encloses, well guarded—connote the presence of arms, or of a state. The sea "holds them." Such a verb on its own may sound maternal; in the context of the other choices, however, it becomes an action of restraint or armed protection. The space for the yachts, then, is rarefied. The land protects the yachts from an ocean that is "ungoverned," and late in the poem it is no coincidence that the ungoverned space is also the space wherein arms and bodies are engaged in dream-like struggle.

The ocean "when it chooses/ tortures the biggest hulls" and must therefore be navigated and controlled by the strongest and most fit. The "best man" is sent up against it, to "pit against its beatings" lest the yachts be sunk. By the fifth line, the relationships are set, so that the poem makes it clear that the yachts rise above and against the ungoverned, and it is the best who pilot them.

In the sixth line, the yachts themselves are first characterized as insect like, a characterization that persists through the early stanzas.

"Mothlike" and "scintillant," the yachts are delicate, able to fly, in some ways indiscernible, yet with "broad bellying sails." The bottoms of the yachts, where the men are, are scarcely seen. Instead, the persona describes the great means of their flight, the sails and the prows that cut the water. Against that greatness the men are "ant like," grounded, small, industrious, and not at all like moths. As the men are described, so are their actions, in a tumult of phrases that mimics the swift action of the crew against the sea, all scarcely visible from shore, where all that is seen is a seemingly calm and billowing sail, something scarcely attainable as it goes "for the mark." The mark is a prize that is given no further definition in the poem. As the syntax mimics the controlled chaos of the race, the lack of definition regarding the mark perfectly characterizes what the pilots wish to attain. To the viewer, it is not something to which he is granted access, and so it remains oblique.

Once the race action of a single yacht is described, along with the beauty and clarity of the race days, the poem expands its focus to take in the entirety of the open water, "the well guarded arena," in which there sail a number of boats, "lesser and greater craft" which fall into a hierarchy of size and make. To the viewer, they symbolize freedom of various sorts: youth, rarity, happiness, and the unencumbered mind. The sum is a particular freedom, one not associated with democracy and its trappings but one, the poem reveals, that is associated with the affluence resulting in one's owning a yacht. The narrator has idealized that freedom in his comments. In the fifth, sixth, and seventh stanzas, he rhapsodizes in metaphor and simile about the character of the yachts and that for which they stand.

However, trouble begins to brew. During the rhapsody, the sea becomes moody. That which protected them and guarded them grows restless. The poem was written in the throes of the Great Depression, and Williams, working in industrial Paterson and being familiar with surrounding New Jersey industrial towns, knew firsthand the resentments and devastation of working families. He personally witnessed riots and strikes. These thoughts were no doubt with him when he recalled the yacht races, as his correspondence makes clear. (See the Mariani excerpt that follows.) Thus, in lines 19 and 20, when the sea looks for the "slightest flaw" in the hull and "fails completely," it is the first sign of uprising, a moment that foreshadows the tumult of the final three stanzas. The wind kicks up again in the following line, and in the eighth stanza, the race continues, and the yachts "slip through" the roiling sea, too well-made to be stopped.

Up until the ninth stanza, the syntax of the lines and sentences is convoluted both to mimic the feel of the machinations needed for the yachts to sail, and to convey the sense of complication and association the viewer has with the scene. In the ninth stanza, however, the lines become direct and declarative. The tactic is a typical one in Williams' poems. He is a poet who strove to find poetry in the so-called common voices of his day, and the directness of such dialogues is often manifest in the most direct passages of his work. Williams is also fond of using snippets of those voices in an attempt at cacophony or polyphony, but not in "The Yachts." Rather, the direct voice at the end is so because the last stanzas deal with those bodies that are sacrificed and unseen so that the yachts may pass above.

Arms try to "clutch at the prows." Bodies are "cut aside." There is both agony and despair, and the race is one of "horror." The surreal vision of the sea as an "entanglement of watery bodies" seems at first very different from the "sea which holds them" (line 18). However, both are characterizations of the same thing, and neither is literal. Therefore, the symbolism still works logically; the sea that holds them is comprised of the bodies they overlook. Their recreation is borne on the back of these masses. The bodies are "lost to the world bearing what they cannot hold. Broken," —the line ends to emphasize "Broken."

That the drowning bodies cry out "failing, failing!" could be interpreted as a critique, or simply part of the dream. Many have argued that the final three stanzas are indeed a dream vision, or at least a hyperbole drawn perhaps from an actual drowning. If so, one needs to reconcile the presence of the poet's concern with skill in the last stanzas. The yachts are "skillful" as they pass over, echoing earlier descriptions that they are "well made" (line 24) and that the clutching hands can find no flaw. If the poem is an equation, and its formal aspects could support such a claim, then "The Yachts" reveals that the skilled and flawless are guarded, while the sea, the masses, are uncontrolled and restless, and seek the downfall of the privileged. All of which is complicated by the viewer's seeing in the yachts all to which one could aspire, all the freedoms that could be earned. It is further complicated by the assertion, in line 31, that the masses are already dead, reaching to be taken up to the earthly paradise. As a result, it is not so easy to see the poem as a simple statement of politics. Rather, it is at once image and dream, narrative and lyrical imagination, an excellent example of how Williams brought so much tradition and innovation at once to his art, and how complicated were the pieces that resulted.

"The Yachts"

PAUL MARIANI ON THE LITERARY ANTECEDENTS OF THE POEM

[Paul Mariani is the author of five poetry collections, including *The Great Wheel* and *Salvage Operations: New & Selected Poems*, as well as numerous books of prose, including *A Useable Past: Essays, 1973-1983*, *William Carlos Williams: The Poet and His Critics*, and four biographies, including *William Carlos Williams: A New World Naked*. He is Distinguished University Professor at the University of Massachusetts, Amherst, where he has taught since 1968. In the excerpt, Mariani uses biographical sources to enumerate the influences on the poem.]

And "The Yachts," that often anthologized, uncharacteristic effort of Williams', which Williams liked though he knew its technique was imitative. He had begun it with Dante's *terza rima* since he was borrowing the scene from the *Inferno* where Dante and Virgil must cut through the arms and hands of the damned floating beneath them who try to sink their small boat. Williams was remembering the magnificent America's Cup yacht races he had seen off Newport, Rhode Island, and the ambivalence he had felt watching all that aristocratic skill while knowing that it was a nation of poor people who in reality supported this small privileged class. In a letter he wrote in late August of that year to Pound, after "The Yachts" had already been printed in the *New Republic*, Williams provided an extraordinary gloss on the sentiments expressed in that poem. The letter was written from Woods Hole, Massachusetts, where Williams had taken Floss and Paul to visit young Bill, who was working in marine biology at the laboratories there for the summer.

Williams had just finished reading Pound's latest book, *Jefferson and/or Mussolini*, and had enjoyed it because Pound had persisted "in finding a local solution pertinent to the present world situation." But Italy was not America, and Williams believed now that the revolution in America was further off than ever. At that moment the trouble with Americans getting anything like justice served to them, as far as Williams was concerned, was "the organized opposition by the wealthy Republicans to everything Roosevelt is trying to do. It's a race: he'll do it his way, putting over the rudiments of an idea, or they'll get the whip hand back and kill the idea." And if the moneyed Republicans did get power, any chance of a revolution would be dead. Williams had called it a race: a political race between Democrats and Republicans like those yachts racing for the America's Cup in the summer of '35. One or the other side would win—probably the special interests once again—and the *sansou*, the poor, the disenfranchised, would be cut aside relentlessly as they clawed against the boats struggling simply to stay afloat:

> *Now the waves strike at them but they are too*
> *well made, they slip through, though they take in canvas.*
>
> *Arms with hands grasping seek to clutch at the prows.*
> *Bodies thrown recklessly in the way are cut aside.*
> *It is a sea of faces about them in agony, in despair*
>
> *until the horror of the race dawns staggering the mind,*
> *the whole sea become an entanglement of watery bodies*
> *lost to the world bearing what they cannot hold. Broken,*
>
> *beaten, desolate, reaching from the dead to be taken up*
> *they cry out, failing, failing! their cries rising*
> *in waves still as the skillful yachts pass over.*

—Paul Mariani, *William Carlos Williams: A New World Naked* (New York: W.W. Norton and Company, 1981): pp. 370-371.

STEPHEN E. WHICHER ON THE TOUGH, PSYCHOLOGICAL JUMBLE OF WILLIAMS

[Stephen E. Whicher is the author of *Freedom and Fate: An Inner Life of Ralph Waldo Emerson*, the co-editor of *The Early Lectures of Ralph Waldo Emerson*, and editor of *Emerson: An Organic Anthology*. In this piece connecting the "difficult" poetries of Cummings, Williams, and Stevens, Whicher makes the case that Williams' poetry, as anti-intellectual as the others, was governed by a "subjective logic" that joined disparate voices in making sense of the jumbled world he knew.]

Perhaps one reason for Williams' strength is the discipline of his profession, since he has combined a career as a poet with a busy professional life as a doctor in Paterson, New Jersey, often working with the poorest kind of patients and seeing the biological facts of life as a doctor must, without a protecting veil of sentiment and illusion. The resulting toughness, without making him callous, has sinewed his verse.

His ruling objective has been to build a poetry of American speech. He regards this aim, correctly enough, as a continuation of the revolt against tradition initiated by Whitman and is probably Whitman's greatest admirer among contemporary poets. Like Whitman, he insists vigorously on the special task of the American poet, to the point of sounding a bit old-fashioned in a time when the American poet has left behind the adolescent need to stress his difference. Where Carl Sandburg, sharing such convictions, has adopted something like Whitman's manner, however. Williams has rejected Whitman's practice for one built on the "free verse" of the Imagist school that flourished briefly under Pound's leadership. He also seeks "direct treatment of the 'thing'" and the rhythm "of the musical phrase, not the metronome." He has become, among other things, a kind of modern Robert Herrick in that, like the Imagists, he is willing to trust the exactness of his notation of some small fact to raise it without comment to poetic significance. His main concern, however, has been to render the peculiar music inherent in American speech habits and to develop without regard to the traditions of a foreign literature the forms proper to that music. Often the line divisions of his poems are little more than a device to force the reader to move through an apparently prosaic statement slowly enough to notice each of its rhythmic elements and savor its unique cadence. Like Robert Frost, he is willing to jettison the "poetic" in order to get us to hear the poetry inherent in the actual.

Like Frost also, he risks and sometimes deserves the verdict, "This is not poetry." He is nevertheless a major poet because, on the one hand, he often expertly discharges the obligation to lift speech into music, and, on the other, because his poems do more than capture fact, whether speech or image; they catch the glancing movements of the creating mind itself, are *psychological* notations worked up into artistic wholes, and thus hold the mirror up to a sensibility which turns out to be an unusually interesting one. "Sensibility," for Williams is not interesting as a thinker; he is as unintellectual as Whitman, and the thought in his verse, like the thought in O'Neill's plays, only exposes the author. But the vigor and subtlety with which the sensibility that controls these poems leaps from image to image, voice to voice, according to a strong subjective logic deep below the surface gives them the kind of depth and power which only a superior poet can command. The best illustration of this power is in the early books of Williams' long poem, *Paterson*, where in the manner of Pound's *Cantos*, by a musical interweaving of themes and images, he attempts with sometimes impressive success to create an order from the thundering chaos of his contemporary America.

The following lyric illustrates some of these qualities. Beginning as an admiring description of racing boats, or yachts, it moves suddenly as the race starts into a surrealistic vision of the "horror of the race." The eye, if not the ear, can notice how touches of rhyme and illiteration subtly accent the expert rhythmic pattern. The title is part of the poem.

—Stephen E. Whicher, *The Art of Poetry: Cummings, Williams, Stevens* (Isle of Skye: Aquila Publishing, 1982): pp. 5-10.

CARL RAPP ON THE PATHETIC FALLACY'S CENTRALITY
TO WILLIAMS' WORK

[Carl Rapp is Professor of English at the University of Georgia. He is the author of *William Carlos Williams and Romantic Idealism* and *Fleeing the Universal*. He has held a Mellon Foundation Lectureship at Brown University. Rapp discusses the importance of the pathetic fallacy to Williams' development of poetics, as well as to the development of the poet's own presence in the work, using the poem as one example.]

In "The Yachts," one of the most spectacular examples of pathetic fallacy occurs when Williams describes how the "moody" sea becomes "an entanglement of watery bodies" in the form of waves (or arms) "with hands grasping" which "seek to clutch at the prows" of the yachts (*CEP*, 106–07). There is nothing incidental about the device, either. It is absolutely fundamental to Williams' whole way of thinking, and examples of it, both serious and whimsical, are legion throughout his poetry. *Paterson*, for that matter, is a gigantic pathetic fallacy based on the assumption that any city may be regarded as the extended embodiment of a man, "all the details of which may be made to voice his most intimate convictions" (*P*, 3). Thus the people of Paterson, New Jersey, are said to be the "thoughts" of the giant N. F. Paterson (*P*, 18), while Williams' own poetry is said to be an attempt to interpret the "voice" or "speech" of the Falls, a speech that is paralleled in the inarticulate (though, at the same time, curiously expressive) behavior that comes pouring out of Paterson's citizens.

—Carl Rapp, *William Carlos Williams and Romantic Idealism* (Hanover: Brown University Press/University Press of New England, 1984): pp. 91-92.

JANET SULLIVAN ON THE DISPARATE VIEWPOINTS AND TACTICS OF CONFUSION IN THE POEM

[In the excerpt, Sullivan describes how the confusion of the poems seemingly two different views of reality are actually rooted in a Blake device.]

In Williams' 1935 "The Yachts" (*Selected Poems,* 71–72), he uses what can be perceived as another variety of tactical difficulty to create an even more intense confusion for the reader when he breaks his poem into two pieces of visual description that appear at first to be based on two entirely different views of reality. Here his subjects and use of pronouns are steady and unambiguous except on the far side of the break, but the very violence of the break and our inability to put the pieces together based on our experience of seeing in the real world—an experience encouraged by the vivid detail of the first part—force us to seek an explanation in symbolism. But here again, the poet encourages our assumption that a feeling "I" is masterminding our experience, in this case by means of a rather Blakean maneuver. In fact, the speaker refers to that controlling mind, however obliquely, throughout, but especially in the second-to-last stanza. Our problems in seeing a magnificent yacht race described in lavish and pleasurable detail in the first eight stanzas turn into a hideous scene of mass drowning in the last three are finally resolved when the speaker explains:

> It is a sea of faces about them in agony, in despair
>
> until the horror of the race dawns staggering the mind,
> the whole sea become an entanglement of watery bodies
> lost to the world bearing what they cannot hold. (ll. 27–30)

—Janet Sullivan, "Encountering the Unicorn: William Carlos Williams and Marianne Moore," *Sagetrieb* 6:3 (1987): pp. 148-149.

BARRY AHEARN ON THE POEM'S PLACE IN WILLIAMS' ATTITUDE TOWARD THE WORKING CLASS

[In this excerpt, near the conclusion of the chapter "Social Diffraction," Ahearn places the poem in the context of Williams' other work on the working classes, articulating Williams' unusual "respectful distance" from them as a poet and professional.]

During the twenties and thirties, Williams never tried to convince himself that he was at heart one of the working class, as did some other poets. His stance remains one of respectful distance. He may sympathize with members of the lower class, but he is not of them. Williams continued to encounter those less fortunate than himself, but the evidence of the poetry indicates that those encounters continued to be in terms of the relation between doctor and patient, or employer and employee. Williams's most famous defense of the lower class, "The Yachts" (CP1, 388-9), notes the "cries" of the oppressed, but does not articulate them. Even such extended passages as the "Sunday in the Park" section of *Paterson*, in which the strolling poet notes the crowd of working-class people present, provides very few examples of their speech. Only in Book Four of *Paterson*, in the voice of Phyllis, do we find the common speech displayed at length. Even here, however, most of that speech again appears in the context of the relation between employer (Corydon) and employee (Phyllis). Williams understood that his birth, education and profession made it virtually impossible for him to enter the mind of the lower class, and he wisely chose not to try.

—Barry Ahearn, *William Carlos Williams and Alterity: The Early Poetry* (New York: Cambridge University Press, 1994): pp.79.

"The Wanderer"

Ezra Pound, Williams' friend and associate, first published "The Wanderer" in his small magazine, *The Egoist*. According to letters, Pound published the poem because he recognized a political leaning to which he, Pound, was sympathetic. The poem has become important to scholars and critics of Williams for reasons beyond the relatively minor political aspects of the poem. Rather, the poem is one of Williams' first to seriously break from his very early and largely imitative lyric and Romantic work. As well, it is the first time he seriously mines his home for a large poetic work. To many critics, "The Wanderer" shows the beginnings of what would, several poetic stabs and twenty-four years later, become the epic *Paterson*.

The poem is subtitled "A Rococo Study," and the reference could refer to the actual Rococo movement in art and architecture that emerged in the latter half of the eighteenth century, or the larger sense of Rococo which implies ornate and artistic qualities and an antiquated manner. Given that the poem was not completed until 1917, the Rococo mention likely is meant to refer to the more general meaning, which would stand in stark contrast to the stated aims of the bolstering movement that would come to be known as Modernism.

The qualities of such a study are hence inherent in the poem. "The Wanderer" is long and ornate, consisting of seven sections, each section of at least a few stanzas. The stanza and section lengths are irregular, further complicating it. The poem is narrative at points, but borrows heavily from the Romantic tradition for its supernatural elements, and from Williams' own Imagist ideas for much of the poem's use of stark description. Three voices work through the poem: the interior monologue of the narrator, his spoken dialogue, and the dialogue of the old woman who serves as his guide.

In the first section, *Advent*, the narrator relates how he first sensed the guide he will follow throughout the poem. He "had no certain knowledge of her" but was aware of her flight above him, comparing her to a crow that skimmed the forests of New Jersey near the Passaic and, further, the Hudson. As he sees her, he imagines he follows in flight (line 10), and he foresees what he will have to endure to gain her knowledge. Thus, his quest is begun.

The biggest question the narrator has to face is "How shall I be a mirror to this modernity?" The question itself occupies a whole line, one of the few complete grammatical sentences to be confined to a single line in the entire poem. Just as he is crossing the ferry into Manhattan, in a moment reminiscent of Whitman and Dante, among others, he sees her, above a "yielding river." He describes the river as such to connote its malleability in accommodating the boats and his travel, but also to foreshadow the eventual yielding of knowledge by the Passaic in a later section of the poem. After the guide calls attention to her own strength (lines 23-26), the narrator sees a gull veer off. The bird is presumably the form the guide wishes to take. To the narrator, the vision is, in his mind, imbued with the divine. "All the persons of godhead" follow the veer of the guide. He thus ascribes to her deific powers, or at least the power to influence the gods.

In *Clarity*, the narrator begins his first work to answer the question posed in the opening section. They are now both gulls soaring above the landscape and the river, and the narrator realizes "one face is all the world." He is referring to the guide, and what he perceives as her agelessness or, rather, her possession of all ages. She is a representation of the modernity of the times, all ages compressed into the knowledge of the current age, "Indifferent, out of sequence, marvelously!" He quickly clarifies to say that the only sequence in which the ages do exist is the one "Which is the beauty of all the world," again seeing the world, very clearly, as she wishes him to. He states as much in line 33 and especially in lines 47 and 48: "It is she/ The mighty, recreating the whole world."

In the stanza following his realizing she is revealing the world through her vision, he understands the worship of those things that comprise the world. Here, however, he equates that appreciation with natural non-human items only: "A red leaf that falls upon a stone!" He is not, at this point, seeing the world as one of humans. He is still seeing humans as something *other* on the world. This only becomes apparent later in the poem. At this point, his clarity causes him to appreciate the items of the world "taking shape before me for worship." So it is a contradiction when, in lines 53 to 64, he describes how his guide is "imperious in beggary." She wears rings that have lost the stones, and a single chain among others that is gold. She is adorned, but only in things that were once great but are no more. She, like that which adorns her, carries the sad trappings of bygone greatness, and to the narrator, there is a glory in that renunciation. When he says "'I will take my peace in her henceforth!'" he is seeking union, to be in her, to be as one. The sexual overtones are complicated by the narrator's search for enlightenment and a view of the world, such that the joining could exist on several levels. His search for union and his gradual shift from the appreciation of things to the appreciation of people foretells that the union will necessarily be more than physical.

In the next three sections, after having taken flight, the guide brings the narrator to Broadway, Paterson, and the cluttered swamps and marshes around Hackensack. The narrator comes upon people in each place. At first, on Broadway, he sees crowds with "expressionless, animate faces," and they seem to have a purpose in their "jostling," but are in fact "Hasting—nowhere!" This contrasts with the later image he has of strikers in Paterson, in lines 130 to 155. In the Paterson section, he describes the bodies of the people in detail, even their "rasping vices, filthy habits." He sees they are united in their want of "a few luxuries," and that they have purpose. He says, "'Nowhere/ The subtle! Everywhere the electric!'" In so doing, he equates the people's lives with the violent and strangely positive phenomenon of electricity. Even though he is "hot for savagery" he finds something more in those whom he witnesses.

In the sections *Paterson—The Strike* and *Abroad*, the guide rebukes the narrator. She rejects his admiration of her, even though he is "sickened" when he smells her sweat, and even though he realizes in lines 71 through 80 that her youthful allure is artifice and, perhaps, enchantment, he still is astonished when "her voice entered at my eyes" and he still follows her thoughts and guidance. She insists that the people he sees "'*live* I tell you!'" As he praises her vision, she exhorts him to tell others of her union with the particularities of the land in which they live. She says, "For never while you permit them to ignore me/ In these shall the full of my freed voice/ Come grappling the ear with intent!" She insists that the people know of the "ripening fruit within" them.

In this way, the narrator is charged with taking his vision back and communicating it. The scene is but one example of the biblical overtones that echo throughout the piece. That the guide is painted with flight and angelic imagery, however changed with age; that the sections number seven, as Barry Ahearn points out and thus match the creation of the world; that the landscape evoked is a garden, and that the transition between worlds is a river that parts and subsumes the narrator; that the message of the guide is one of morality and almost a call to faith—all of these resonate with religious allusion, a powerful and far less studied aspect of Williams' work, but one that exists in a fine example here.

When in lines 180 through 188, the Eden, that place of innocence within them, is evoked. The plant imagery is echoed later in line 200, when the narrator realizes "But my voice was a seed in the wind." Again, it is another rare complete sentence that also occupies its own line. And again, the sentence is an important one. The Eden within, if you will, that garden place of discovery and innocence that the guide wishes the narrator to awaken in others, is yet nascent in him. His voice is only a seed. His awareness is only growing. As it does, he surveys Hackensack, and sees it "All so old, so familiar—so new now/ To my marveling eyes as we passed/ Invisible."

Soothsay occurs eight days after the night flight over the Hudson River Valley. At this point, the guide offers the narrator a chance to see into the future, to see what he will become in old age. In the guide's conjuring of that age, she repeats several times, "Behold yourself old!" and paints a picture of the guide as "the new Atlas," holding up his fellow man. He is strong for his knowledge, and that strength is made real in the poem by natural imagery. She reveals to him, at the end of the vision, her nature: "Good is my over lip evil/ My underlip to you henceforth:/ For I have taken your soul between my two hands/ And this shall be as it is spoken." The passage is made the more tense with the enjambment after "evil," and Williams' placing of the two on the same line highlights the struggle going on not only in the narrator (of which he is only recently aware) but in the people he observes as well, the people to whom he is to be as an Atlas. The passage could refer to the two lips that comprise the mouth, the source of the telling that the narrator hears. It is also possible that the upper lip is the mouth and that the "underlip" is a sexual reference, combining aspects of mythology that place good and evil in the crone figure, with evil as emanating from the genitals of woman, and good the equivalent of learned advice that is spoken, or of the mouth. Either way, her containing good and evil, as well as stating without mystery that she has shaped the narrator and that her soothsaying will indeed come to pass, works to complete the revelation to the narrator. Additionally, the guides words, "as it is spoke" again have Biblical overtones.

The narrator still seeks a union or transformation, even transcendence. He laments, in *St. James Grove,* that the "novitiate was ended/ The ecstasy was over, the life begun." But his guide has more to come in this final section. The narrator is looking for more and so dresses as though he expects it. He wears a tie given him by his grandmother, an allusion that suggests the guide shares much with the grandmother. (Critics have even suggested that the guide is meant to be Emily Dickinson Wellcome, the poet's grandmother.) They arrive finally at "The Passaic, that filthy river." The river is once more in the section referred to as the filthy Passaic, in a stanza of one line where it is set off, underscoring the narrator's refusal, given his new knowledge, to romanticize that which is around him. Yet, importantly, in the scene that follows, that river, with its filth and copiousness, is the very agent of his transcendence. The woman only led him there.

She bathes his brow, and so he is baptized in the realism of filth. She calls on the river, which is old like her. She asks that the river give him "the well-worn spirit," calling for "the old friend of my revels." She has a likeness in mind, which may well be the river. The river, of course, becomes important as a source for Williams' later poetry, for his break from romanticizing in his outlook as well as in his poems. After she calls it, the river enters the narrator, through his heart. He has been baptized, and now the river enters his very core. As it does, the narrator feels "the utter depth of its rottenness/ The vile breadth of its degradation" and he drops down "knowing this was me now." The word down characterizes the realization of descent, of going into oneself, of acknowledging lower and baser parts of the self. But the guide does not let him rest or wallow in his baser self. She lifts him, and the river fights within him until "its last motion had ceased/ And I knew all—and it became me." The line recalls Whitman's grand claim to contain multitudes. Here, the narrator, the poet, states that a poet must contain it all. The following line (line 387) continues the passage, and as it does the narrator sees his self, his new realization, drifting away in the river. On finding himself, he risks losing himself to the very agent of change.

His guide knows the change is necessary. While the narrator watches his self being borne away, she averts her eyes. When he notices, the transcendence is complete. He is aware of the change, aware of her role and his complicity in his own change, and the river itself is the manifestation of that awareness. When the last of him is taken, she turns to the river and casts a spell, stating that their baptism shall leave a sanctuary beside the river. Their sacrifice—the fate of wandering and continuing to search for self in the particularities of their place—will sanctify the place where it began. It "shall be a bird's paradise," thus continuing the imagery of the guide from earlier. The most "secluded places" will be "hallowed by a stench/ To be our joint solitude and temple." She asks then that the river remember their new son, the product of the guide and the river itself, and the paradox of its awful and filthy knowledge which sends the narrator, the poet, on the "new wandering," the quest to let people discover the knowledge and garden within themselves as he does the same.

The fantastical and quasi-religious ending brings together many themes that continued to work through Williams' work in the years that followed: the attention to the local and the tangible things that comprise it; his attention to the working classes; his development of the female as important to both the artistic vision and a complete temperament; and the iconography of religion and the natural world. All of those themes found their highest expression in Williams' crowning achievement, *Paterson*, having had their genesis here, by the side of the filthy Passaic, in "The Wanderer."

"The Wanderer"

RICHARD A. MACKSEY ON THE POEM AS WILLIAMS' FIRST MAJOR STYLISTIC TRANSITION

[Richard A. Macksey is a writer and critic who has taught at Johns Hopkins University since 1958, holding a joint appointment in the Humanities Center and in the Writing Seminars. He is the editor of the journal *MLN,* and has also edited or co-edited *Velocities of Change: Critical Essays from MLN, Consequences of Enlightenment,* and *Language of Criticism and the Sciences of Man: The Structuralist Controversy.* Macksey reveals how the poem expands beyond the restrictions of Williams' Imagist background and moves into more lyric and contemplative work.]

"So he went on, homeward or seeking a home that was his own, all this through a 'foreign' country whose language was barbarous" (*A,* 60).

Nothing could be further removed from the project of a poet who championed the local and immediate. The hero's separation was as total as his author's frustration, which grew while "book followed book," until the frantic young poet finally managed to dispatch the manuscript through the furnace door. Starting from a new beginning, as the *Autobiography* testifies, Williams underwent the first genuine rite of passage immediately thereafter. He turned to a new conception of poetry in the very act of writing the next poem.

This first surviving long poem, "The Wanderer," carries him beyond the alienation implied by the title and records a total immersion. Under the tutelary spirit of his formidable grandmother the hero plunges into the filth of the Passaic River. (Sister Bernetta Quinn had to remind the poet that this was the source which was ultimately to flow into the creation of *Paterson.*) The hero celebrates a ritual marriage from which he emerges refreshed and miraculously possessed of his world. Unlike the earlier Keatsian wanderings, this voyage, in its absolute submission and possession, brings him home.

What flows from this ritual sacrifice of his isolation is the concrete richness of Williams' "imagist" poetry, where the sensuous "contours and the shine/hold the eye" as the "Sea-Trout and Butterfish" dart into sharp definition, separated from the watery matrix:

> The eye comes down eagerly
> unravelled of the sea
>
> separates this from that
> and the fine fins' sharp spines   (CEP, 91)

And yet, in his intensely personal acceptance and affirmation of this world of particulars, Williams has already moved beyond the chastity of the orthodox imagist. His hardness and concentration in the best poems of this period bear the unique mark of his own hand pressing out and touching.

This constant pressure of the poet's identity, responding to the fecund variety of things in the very act of discovering and exploring them, is one clue to the profound assurance as a sensate part of the immediate world which Williams firmly achieved after the nuptial plunge into the filth of the Passaic River. He acknowledges this ritual transition into secure community with other things in an important letter to his friend Marianne Moore:

> The inner security though is an overwhelmingly important observation. . . . It is something which occurred once when I was about twenty, a sudden resignation to existence, a despair—if you wish to call it that, but a despair which made everything a unit and at the same time a part of myself. I suppose it might be called a sort of nameless religious experience. I resigned, I gave up. . . . I won't follow causes. I can't. The reason is that it seems so much more important to me that I am. Where shall one go? What shall one do? Things have no names for me and places have no significance. As a reward for this anonymity I feel as much a part of things as trees and stones. Heaven seems frankly impossible. I am damned as I succeed. I have no particular hope save to repair, to rescue, to complete.   (SL, 147)

Williams thus describes his point of departure, without baggage but totally at home in a world which he can both heal and sustain.

—Richard A. Macksey, "'A Certainty of Music:' Williams' Changes." In *William Carlos Williams: A Collection of Critical Essays* (Englewood Cliffs: Prentice-Hall, Inc., 1966): pp. 141-142.

CARL RAPP ON WILLIAMS' USE OF ROMANTICISM AND IDEALISM

[In the excerpt, taken from a longer chapter that outlines the poem as an allegory of Williams' development as a poet, Rapp argues that Williams has not neglected the very traditions of poetry he is said to have transcended.]

Since "The Wanderer" is the poem which is supposed to express Williams' departure from all these traditions, it serves as an appropriate starting point. One important question that needs to be answered is this: How can a poem so obviously dependent on Keats be said to precipitate its author beyond romanticism? The prevailing view of "The Wanderer" makes sense, I think, only if the exuberant Whitman-like affirmation of "this" world, with which the poem concludes, is really anti-Keatsian or antiromantic. In fact, it is not. However much "The Wanderer" reminds one of Whitman's poems ("Crossing Brooklyn Ferry," for example, or "This Compost"), the true inspiration behind it seems to have been Keats's Hyperion fragments. And, if we look closely at these poems, we find that Williams' poem does not imply anything essentially different from what they imply about the nature of the poet and the objects of the poet's experience. Whether he knew it or not, in writing "The Wanderer," Williams was affirming an essentially romantic conception of his own vocation.

"The Wanderer" is the story of the development of Williams' awareness of himself as a poet. In his relationship to the ugly goddess who acts as his mentor in the poem, the narrator recapitulates the relationship between Apollo and Mnemosyne in "Hyperion" and also, of course, the relationship between the narrator and Moneta in "The Fall of Hyperion." As Williams' poem begins, the narrator finds himself facing the same problem his Keatsian counterparts face: he is not altogether sure who he is or what his place is to be in the world around him. Crossing the ferry into New York, he sees before him "the great towers of Manhattan," and he asks himself rather diffidently, "How shall I be a mirror to this modernity?" (*CEP*, 3). This question suggests at the very outset that the fledgling poet who asks it has not yet found a satisfactory way to relate himself to the external world, particularly the world of the city. That he desires at least some sort of relation is evident from the fact that he is already moving in the direction of "the great towers." Quite suddenly, however, he is distracted from his thoughts by the appearance of a strange goddess who calls to him from the water, and then, unaccountably, disappears into the sky in the form of "a great seagull." Dazzled and excited, the young poet-to-be turns away from the city, his original destination, to pursue the goddess:

> "Come!" cried my mind and by her might
> That was upon us we flew above the river
> Seeking her, grey gulls among the white—
> *(CEP,* 4)

From this point on in the poem, the goddess alone—not the city—becomes the object of his concentrated attention:

> "I am given," cried I, "now I know it!
> I know now all my time is forespent!
> For me one face is all the world!
> For I have seen her at last, this day,
> In whom age in age is united—
> Indifferent, out of sequence, marvelously!
> Saving alone that one sequence
> Which is the beauty of all the world, for surely
> Either there in the rolling smoke spheres below us
> Or here with us in the air intercircling,
> Certainly somewhere here about us
> I know she is revealing these things!
> And as gulls we flew and with soft cries
> We seemed to speak, flying, "It is she
> The mighty, recreating the whole world,
> This is the first day of wonders!
> *(CEP,* 4)

Williams (or the narrator) apparently takes the goddess to be a kind of logos that manifests itself in all things as a single principle. The ambiguity of her status, however, makes him conceive of her as an alternative to the "modernity" that previously concerned him, and so he declares: "I will take my peace in her henceforth!" When she turns his attention back to the city in the third section of the poem, he finds it repellent:

There came crowds walking—men as visions
With expressionless, animate faces;
Empty men with shell-thin bodies
Jostling close above the gutter,
Hasting—nowhere!

(CEP, 5)

Just at this moment, he sees her for the first time as she really is—
"ominous, old, painted"—a ghastly figure of a woman, yet strangely alluring.

> —Carl Rapp, *William Carlos Williams and Romantic Idealism*
> (Hanover: Brown University Press/University Press of New England,
> 1984): pp. 6-8.

ANDREW LAWSON ON THE WANDERER AS OUTCAST

> [Andrew Lawson studied English at Leeds University and
> did postgraduate work at Oxford University in American
> Literature. He currently is on staff at Staffordshire
> University. He is writing a book on class identity and mod-
> ern American writing. Lawson's essay discusses political
> concerns of the day (and of the movement) and how the
> poem represented and reacted to them. In the excerpt in par-
> ticular, Lawson argues with early readings of the poem,
> placing the poem's persona distinctly outside of society
> despite of the poem's themes of immersion, baptism, and
> transcendence.]

The title of the poem refers to Pound's adoption of the theme of the
wanderer, with his recent translation of the Anglo-Saxon "Seafarer,"
and his promotion of the Provençal troubadours where the poet is
positioned radically outside of society, but able to petition an ideal
beauty. Williams's Wanderer is a poet figure, an intellectual representative of what Georges Santayana described in 1913, as "the
Wandrejahre of Faith," the period of cultural revaluation which saw
the twilight of the idols of gentility and the birth of new, modern
gods (Santayana, 13). It was becoming a commonplace for
Progressive radicals and intellectuals to describe their own alienation from the norms of American life in terms of homelessness and

wandering. One of the most astute cultural critics of the period, Walter Lippmann described in 1914 his search for emancipated alternatives to the Victorian shibboleths of "the sanctity of property, the patriarchal family, hereditary caste, the dogma of sin, obedience to authority, "as a state of 'drift' requiring theoretical 'mastery'" (Lippmann, xvii). "We have lost authority," Lippmann wrote, "we are 'emancipated' from an ordered world. We drift. . . . We are homeless in a jungle of machines and untamed powers that haunt the imagination. Of course, our culture is confused, our thinking spasmodic, and our emotions out of kilter" (196–7). Randolph Bourne complained in 1915 of his "deviation from the norm of popular music, the movies, [R. M.] Chamber[s]'s novels, Billy Sunday, musical comedy, tennis, anti-suffragism" of his "middle-middle class" family: "My relatives are quite hopeless, and I feel at times like a homesick wanderer, not even knowing where my true home is" (Qtd. Lasch 79). Williams's poem, with its ersatz Romantic dreamvision, captures exactly that sense of suspension in a historical interregnum, the "dreaming quality of life" described by Lippmann and Bourne, the feeling of homesickness and nostalgia for a past that never actually existed: "Too far ahead there is nothing but your dream; just behind, there is nothing but your memory" (Lippmann, xxii–xxiii). More than that, however, it starts to ask how this condition of drifting might be halted, and its ambivalences and discontinuities turned to pragmatic critical effect.

—Andrew Lawson, "Divisions of Labour: William Carlos Williams's 'The Wanderer' and the Politics of Modernism." *William Carlos Williams Review* 20 (Spring 1994): pp. 5.

BRUCE COMENS ON THE POEM'S POWER AS APOCALYPTIC PREDICTION

[This excerpt argues that the poem, contrary to what past critics have said, is not a statement of union or of poetic omniscience, but rather is recognition of the fleeting nature of the physical present, and the poet's realization that such a union is elusive. Comens claims that as such, it foresees apocalypse as the only way to achieve union.]

the narrator's formal claim to omniscience—"And I knew all"—to the colloquial, "And I knew this for double certain." Not only does the tonal shift undermine the earlier claim, but "knowing all" suddenly depends on being "double certain," which undermines this omniscience even further. The subsequent doubling of the narrator also marks an ironic distance surfacing under the guise of his ecstatic union. And finally, he seems to take the notion of a religious ecstasy, a standing outside oneself—a death of the self—rather too literally when he sees his own pale, drowned corpse floating off in the river, submerged in the "all."

The narrator's quest, then, results only in the knowledge that the quest itself is useless, in many respects a fraud: the apocalyptic vision is inadequate or even irrelevant. At the end of the poem, the "marvelous old queen" bids goodbye to the river in terms that stress its existence in a fantastic realm—fertile, rich in vegetation and life, "a bird's paradise"—a realm wholly apart from human lives and for that matter from the real Passaic. And so the narrator is finally left with nothing but "the new wandering," which is "new" in only two respects: first, this wandering is not linear, it proceeds to no fixed goal, and second, there is no possibility of escape from it, either through transcendence or immanence. "The Wanderer," then, is on the surface a quintessential strategic poem: not only does it recount a past experience from a secure, eternal position, rendering a preconceived narrative in verse (which is to say, using language transparently, instrumentally), but it recounts the very experience that should have given the poet a secure basis from which to deploy his strategies, his discourse. In fact, however, the related experience negates the possibility of such a basis and projects the poet-narrator forward into a world of loss, where there can be no secure self, anchored in a vision of the divine—a world where there can only be tactics. Where Pound was at this time developing a poetics of fragmentation, seemingly tactical but actually displaying an underlying, strategic basis, Williams makes tactical use of a traditional strategy. "The Wanderer" does not achieve an apocalypse; it uses the form of revelation to point to a condition where such forms, such desires, will be abandoned. In a sense, the poem says goodbye to all that, but has not itself left. Because the poet-wanderer can find no place in the present, he can only project a future poetics of tactics that will eschew his own current reliance on a traditional strategy.

—Bruce Comens, *Apocalypse and After: Modern Strategy and Postmodern Tactics in Pound, Williams, and Zukofsky* (Tuscaloosa: University of Alabama Press, 1995): pp. 89-92

BARRY AHEARN ON TRANSFORMATION AND OTHER VOICES IN THE POEM

[Here Ahearn discusses how the poem is one of transformation, particularly the poet's, since it contains so many imitations of other voices.]

Williams also considers metamorphosis that goes beyond the physical; some of his longest poems from the early years center around spiritual transformation. In "The Wanderer" (*CP1*, 108–17) he finds himself on the border between Rutherford and Manhattan. In this zone between the two poles of his existence, he first sees the female deity who instructs him. The echo of Whitman here is not so much "Crossing Brooklyn Ferry," but "Out of the Cradle Endlessly Rocking," the poem in which the young poet first learns of his vocation while standing on the margin between sea and land. Other poets, texts and mannerisms are detectable in "The Wanderer": Yeats, whose vocabulary appears in patches ("The high wanderer of by-ways / Walking imperious in beggary!"—*CP1*, 109); the Bible (the creation of the world in seven days is echoed in the seven parts of the poem); Baudelaire and Poe (in the urban vision of "Broadway" and its horror at the "crowds walking"); Keats in the appeal the poet makes at the end of "Broadway" for the goddess to instruct him in the secrets of the hearts of the city dwellers (the precedent is the "Ode on Melancholy," where Keats conceives of knowledge as acquired not through direct contact but through the mediation of the goddess). The overall pattern of the journey with the instructing spirit, which begins in the second part of the poem, suggests nothing so much as the tours conducted by the Yuletide spirits of Dickens's *A Christmas Carol*. It is an appropriate model for Williams because it tells the story of the profound psychological transformation of the protagonist and because it combines urban and rural (Scrooge's school days) settings.

Williams's own urge for transformation at the end of "Broadway" seems a desire for the fate of Orpheus—namely, dissolution. That would certainly be a form of metamorphosis, but only one of escape. The goddess conducting Williams will not permit it. Behind his desire for an attachment to the protean goddess, expressed as a plea to be allowed to be "'carried / Whatever way the head of your whim is, / A burr upon those streaming tatters'" (*CP1*, 111), may be a desire to lose one's identity in that of the maternal deity. The poem emphasizes the appeal of the maternal in the next section, "The Strike," in which the abhorrent industrial scene figures as paternal roughhousing: 'Ugly, venomous, gigantic! / Tossing me as a great father his helpless / Infant till it shriek with ecstasy / And its eyes roll and its tongue hangs out!—'" (*CP1*, 112). The transformation that the goddess allows Williams becomes clear in the last section, "Abroad." The goddess charges the poet with being her prophet to the unhearing. There are Whitmanian echoes (specifically of "Out of the Cradle Endlessly Rocking") in the repetition of such words as "never" and "waken" in this section. But the content of her charge seems Wordsworthian; she instructs him to tell humankind of natural elements in the human world, such as "the silent phoebe nest / Under the eaves of your spirit" (*CP1*, 113).

On the whole, "The Wanderer" is an excellent pastiche of other poets' motifs and styles. It also expresses Williams's deep-seated restlessness in his present form and occupations. But it makes no technical advance. It expresses a desire for change in an old-fashioned language. Even if Williams did undergo a dramatic spiritual illumination, he has not yet invented the language that could adequately record such a rebirth.

—Barry Ahearn, *William Carlos Williams and Alterity: The Early Poetry* (New York: Cambridge University Press, 1994): pp. 119-120.

ALEC MARSH ON WILLIAMS AS A MIRROR TO MODERNITY

[Alec Marsh is Assistant Professor of English at Muhlenberg College. *Money and Modernity* is his first book. In the excerpt, taken from a longer sub-section dealing with the poem, Marsh discusses how the poem shows Williams' early development of his ideas on the poet's perspective, and the importance of philosopher John Dewey to those ideas.]

Williams chooses Whitman as a rival inspiration superior to Keats. [. . .] The Whitman influence abides, to provoke Williams throughout his career. Williams's full "interpretation" of *that* strong precursor will only be completed in *Paterson*—one reason we need to look at "The Wanderer" before turning to the larger poem.

If we take Williams's question, "How shall I be a mirror to this modernity?" as a question that all poets of his generation should have been asking themselves, and if we assume that Williams wanted "The Wanderer" to stand as a kind of answer to the question, then the solution, paradoxically, seems to have involved going back to the past, in this case, to recuperate Whitman's "Crossing Brooklyn Ferry" as a new modern mirror.

Like other American male poets—Hart Crane, for example— Williams sought in Whitman an answer to the inadequacies of the English Romantic tradition that was proving irrelevant to the demands that twentieth-century America was making on the poetic imagination. "The Wanderer," set on the Hudson River ferry, is quite consciously in dialogue with Whitman's poem of the East River crossing. But choosing Whitman as precursor meant rejecting another past represented by the English Romantic poets, specifically Keats. The drama of the poem is in the ephebe's struggle to mediate these competing influences and to realize, as the Scene of his Instruction unfolds, that he must overcome the Keats influence in favor of Whitman's. To put the question in very much broader terms, we could say that the drama of "The Wanderer" is Williams's struggle to choose America over England. In saying this, we say that Williams is embarked on a quest for his own American identity.

In his *Autobiography*, Williams recalls his principal early work, prior to "The Wanderer," as a vast romance, featuring "the aimless wandering . . . of the young prince . . . He went on, homeward or seeking a home that was his own, all this through a 'foreign' country whose language was barbarous." The poem was "poetically descriptive of nature, trees for the most part, 'forests' strange forests—wandering at random, without guide alone" (*A* 60).

Williams's irony lets us know that what appeared to be a foreign country to his young poet-self was, simply, America. The barbarous language was his own American English. Thirty-five years after writing it, Williams clearly interprets "The Wanderer" as his liberation from this "aimless" wandering. The poem frees the young poet from his pose as a foreigner in his own land and from the fruitless task of trying to rewrite Keats rewriting Spenser in *Endymion*. In light of Williams's own reflections, the title of his first important poem may always have been loaded with self-irony. It makes sense, then, that the "guide" Williams discovered in "The Wanderer" is a semicomic Whitman in drag, by turns a crow and a seagull, a "marvelous old queen" (*CP1*, 30), a slattern, an "old crone" (32), and a "beggar" (34). Because she is a necessary ally to Williams in "seizing the precursor's power," she must also be a repressed version, or interpretation, of Keats. Thus she looks as Whitman might look if we could imagine him absurdly dressed as Keats's Moneta in "Hyperion."

This odd figure first appears in the poem as a crow watched by the ephebe:

> I saw her eyes straining in the new distance
> And as the woods fell from her flying
> Likewise they fell from me as I followed—
> So that I knew (that time) what I must put from me
> To hold myself ready for the high course
> (*CP1*, 27)

The woods here are the woods of the Romantic juvenilia that Williams had written hitherto. They represent all that he has already rejected so that he may approach the Scene of Instruction to learn really how to achieve clarity of poetic vision.

The Whitman influence immediately arrives to educate the poet. The ephebe has known what to reject; now he must be taught what to affirm. Whitman, in the form of the gull from "Crossing Brooklyn Ferry," appears as the ephebe is crossing the Hudson River ferry to Manhattan, "wearying many questions" (27), chief among them, "How shall I be a mirror to this modernity?" (28). At that moment the ephebe sees the gull who has flown out of Whitman's poem into his and joins her to fly above the river.

In finding the strength to reject overt English poetic influence, Williams has taken Whitman at his word that "you that shall cross from shore to shore years hence are more to me, and more in my meditations, than you might suppose" (Whitman, 308). Williams's question about the poet's relation to modernity ponders Whitman's mystic faith in "the similitudes of the past and those of the future" (308). Similitude, however, is not identity. The quest in "The Wanderer" is to discover whether Whitman's methods can teach Williams about modernity. But if Whitman is clearly a better choice than Keats as a model for the modern poet, to what degree is the model of Whitman appropriate to modernity? The very need for Williams's question about modernity suggests the changes in American life that required a somewhat different kind of poetic self-consciousness from Whitman's.

—Alec Marsh, *Money and Modernity: Pound, Williams, and the Spirit of Jefferson* (Tuscaloosa: The University of Alabama Press, 1998): pp. 175-177.

"Burning The Christmas Greens"

"Burning the Christmas Greens" is a poem from the latter third of Williams' career, and the latest poem to be considered in this book. Published in the small collection of 1944, *The Wedge*, the poem (and the collection as well, for that matter) is notable for its formal rigidity after the period of line experimentation that dominates Williams' poetry up until the publication of *The Complete Collected Poems of William Carlos Williams* in 1938. The poem is entirely in quatrains (with the exception of the first stanza), and the lines generally have a regular number of stresses, though they are not metrically rigid. The poem addresses, once again, themes of transformation and change, putting to use the familiar items of the life Williams knew well.

The poem opens with an oblique pronoun reference which could be perceived as vague and open, or simply a reference to the title. The enjambment at the end of the first line adds to the disjointed feel of the opening—a feeling that persists into the second line. Williams does not use standard punctuation to place a pause between the first and second line, and the poem thus begins by establishing unusual and charged language. The first stanza highlights the violence of the poem; greens are "cracked and flung," the fire is a "roar."

The following stanza uses repetition of sound and color to intensify the power of the act of burning the greens. That it is essentially a cleansing act is forcefully established here with the repetition of the word "clean" and its sonic match with "green." The repetition will persist throughout the poem, with colors repeating just as "red" appears three times in different comparisons here. Just as clean is evoked for green, the body is evoked for red. The red is blood and living. The flame, which is red, produces the ash. The body, then, becomes transformed. Because the stanza begins by telling the reader "All recognition" is "lost," the greens cease to be greens. In the context of Christmas, the transition then carries with it the overtones of transubstantiation. The flames' appearance as "blood wakes/ on the ash" further suggest that Christian miracle, recalling both the passion of Christ and the blood rites of the new covenant as described in many parts of the New Testament.

The fire serves as the event in the present around which the whole of the poem is built. However, several points in the poem refer to different times and events that are affected relevant to the fire. In the fourth stanza, the narrator recalls the trip to obtain the greens. The group leaves at "the winter's midnight," a reference to the solstice. In line 13, the line ends at "coarse," and while it modifies "holly" on the next line, the enjambment links the word to describe the trees as a whole. In the following stanza, the time is reiterated; it is the "moment of the cold's/ deepest plunge." They cut greens, as it states in line 20, "to fill our need, and over"—another enjambment which suggests the narrator thinks the need the family feels is beyond the cold, beyond the depth of the winter. Given the religious overtones of the earlier lines, and the meditation to come, in late stanzas, and that the enjambment occurs at the beginning of a stanza, one sees that this idea is important to the poem.

The lines which follow point out where the greens are placed, and the words of the stanza highlight the temporary nature of this time in the house. There are "paper Christmas/ bells covered with tinfoil" fastened only by "red ribbons." All is artifice and precariousness, and the line break in line 21 further underscores the fleetingness of the celebration. The red here is not given the attention it gets in the fire. The fire is a particular red, and one of more importance. But in line 27, the green is again the "living green" which has endured a degree of violence. Two lines in the stanza end on "prongs," and "hung."

In the next stanza, the family places white deer among the hemlock sprays, and the narrator recalls how they looked as though they were living. The sight is "gentle and good." But the stanza returns to the present then, after the mention of the living creatures in the artificial wood. "Their time past," he says, is a relief. Something that a few syllables before was good has become something the narrator is glad to see gone. The bareness of the room resonates with the cold of the season.

In the next stanza, the narrator recalls how they "stuffed the dead grate" with the greens, on the "log's smoldering eye" which opened red. They look down at the scene. The eye is behind the grate, a gateway for death, for transformation. The red here is an eye, adding metaphorical weight to the earlier comparisons. As he looks, the poem shifts to a more intensely lyrical mode as the narrator contemplates green. He says "Green is a solace" and " a promise of peace," a shelter. The people burning the greens do not expressly state it, but the narrator suspects they might, as he points out in the parenthetical in lines 46-47. Here, the snow is "hard" but the green provides shelter to birds. Snow becomes "the unseeing bullets of/ the storm." Again, the enjambment highlights the controlled violence of the poem. The birds themselves are as conflicted in the face of the green as is the narrator in his sense of the season; their cries are "plaintive/ rallying" and they hide and yet dodge.

Finally, in line 55, just as the spruce boughs are weighted down to snap under the snow, all is "Transformed!"—the greens, the setting, the poem. The tone of the piece changes, and the first line after the transformation states, "Violence leaped and appeared." The family cowers away from the flame, its sudden power, its light, its flames. Their "eyes recoiled"—averting before power, from the great red eye behind the grate. In the stanza that follows, the transformation is further described, as green goes to red, "instant and alive." The green and all its "sure abutments" are gone. Yet, within the grate, a world appears (line 66), and the black mountains, ash and red, the "infant landscape" recalls imagery of hell.

Even as the viewers are lost in the vision and, "breathless to be witnesses," the narrator is further contemplating what he is seeing. This time, instead of musing on nature or recalling the greens themselves, he is fully engaged with the transformation he has witnessed. The red itself has proven to be life. The green has become the red. There is more than the hell imagery that comprises this world behind the grate. The poem's sudden turn at the end is evidence of the complexity of that transformation. The narrator is overwhelmed and breathless, but it is not out of fear. He states that it feels "as if we stood/ ourselves refreshed among/ the shining fauna of that fire." That it refreshes makes the fire more metaphorical than literal at this point of the poem. In addition, the greens are now part of a "shining fauna." They are no longer flora. They are fauna, a term for all the given animals of a particular region, considered as a whole. The greens are a living, animal world.

"Burning the Christmas Greens," then, contains creation and transformation, and the narrator has been witness to it, at the time of the year when life is most elusive, and those who take part in Christian rites recognize it as a time of wondrous events. Williams here finds such wonder at the season's end, in an act of cleaning that comes to contain more than this narrator ever expected.

"Burning The Christmas Greens"

RICHARD A. MACKSEY ON THE POEM'S TRANSFORMATION

[Richard A. Macksey is a writer and critic who has taught at Johns Hopkins University since 1958, holding a joint appointment in the Humanities Center and in the Writing Seminars. He is the editor of the journal *MLN,* and has also edited or co-edited *Velocities of Change: Critical Essays from MLN, Consequences of Enlightenment,* and *Language of Criticism and the Sciences of Man: The Structuralist Controversy.* In the excerpt, Mackey discusses how the poem negotiates polarities by allowing the physical particulars to be transformed in a fire that can be understood to have a potential multitude of meanings.]

Williams may have learned this montage of times and places on a continuous pictorial plane from the experiments of Gris and the other Cubist painters whom he early championed. As in the "static action" of their painting, everything must be present within the field at once and the poem cannot depend upon any doctrine of correspondence or technique of indirection; the "resonances" must be all present to the view. As early as the Prologue to *Kora in Hell* Williams argued that "the coining of similes is a pastime of very low order, depending as it does upon a nearly vegetable coincidence. Much more keen is that power which discovers in things those inimitable particles of dissimilarity to all other things which are the peculiar perfections of the thing in question" (*SE,* 16). The operative word here is the active verb "discovers," which suggests both the variety and the vigor of Williams' enterprise.

The "peculiar perfections" which the poet discovers are born out of strenuous oppositions (although never the romantic opposition of subject and object). The mind of the poet, that "queer sponge" of which he speaks in "May 1st Tomorrow," assimilates them all and utters them forth again under the vigorous squeezing which is the creative process. The perfection of the flower declares itself against the formless rubble from which it grows: "Milkweed, a single stalk on the bare/embankment" (*CLP*, 28). The male poet or sparrow assertively defines himself as he waltzes before his determined mate. The polarities are founded in a cosmology of elemental opposition between the formless "ground" of anarchic muck and the achieved form of flowers and gestures and poems. Objects are for Williams "nodes of energy" in a field of force. Between the two poles flows the transforming energy, both creative and destructive, of the "radiant gist." It is this daemonic force, an animism in nature and the imagination in the poet, which can convert matter into energy and a desolate field into the vibrant "white desire of Queen-Anne's-Lace. As his insistent floral imagery suggests, for Williams the oppositions can be understood in sexual terms, with the animistic principle, the radioactive "fire," flowing between male and female, between form and matrix, between creation and destruction. The fire is the transforming imagination of the poet entering and commanding, but it is also the flame which releases a new beauty in "Burning the Christmas Greens" and in *Paterson III*, Section 3.

—Richard A. Macksey, "'A Certainty of Music:' Williams' Changes." In *William Carlos Williams: A Collection of Critical Essays* (Englewood Cliffs: Prentice-Hall, Inc., 1966); pp. 136-137.

Roy Harvey Pearce on Williams' "New Mode"

[Roy Harvey Pearce was founder and Chair of the Department of Literature at the University of California, San Diego, as well as founder of the UCSD Archive for New Poetry. He is the author of many books, including *The Continuity of American Poetry*, *The Savages of America / Savagism and Civilization,* and *Hawthorne Centenary Essays*. In the excerpt, Pearce explicates the poem, as well as "The Pink Church," to reveal how Williams uses prosodic techniques to transcend and fuse traditional modes of poetry, thereby creating the "new mode."]

No ideas but in things, as Williams says in *Paterson*—where, writing in both modes at once, he most fully realizes the possibilities of his kind of poem. This is what he called "the new mode." The role of the "line" here is to control and modulate revelation according to the nature and needs of poet and reader, and of the language they share. Both precision of speech and sharpness of vision are subordinated to the movement toward that awareness which is for the poet antecedent to them—their occasion, in fact. Yet we can distinguish between that of which we become aware and ourselves in the act of becoming aware. Mediating between us and the world of the poem, between subject and object, is the poem itself. This should be enough.

Yet Williams has come to want more than this. He would have the poem be the means whereby subject and object are fused. Toward this purpose he has directed the bulk of his poems since *Paterson*. He was, in fact, moving toward it at the time he was working on *Paterson*. There is "Choral: The Pink Church," in which we read:

> Sing!
> transparent to the light
>   through which the light
> shines, through the stone,
>   until
> the stone-light glows,
>   pink jade
> —that is the light and is
>   a stone
> and is a church—if the image
>   hold . . .

"The Pink Church" is the poet's world, and all the persons, places, and things it contains; much of the poem runs, Whitmanlike, over their names, so attempting to absorb them into that ultimate pinkness, that ultimate light, that ultimate revelation, into which a full sense of their presence must issue. Likewise, there is "Burning the Christmas Greens," which begins:

> Their time past, pulled down
> cracked and flung to the fire
> —go up in a roar
>
> All recognition lost, burnt clean
> clean in the flame, the green
> dispersed, a living red,
> flame red, red as blood wakes
> on the ash—

Again, that light which moves as the blood moves. The theme of the poem is put explicitly toward the end:

> . . . Transformed!

> Violence leaped and appeared.
> Recreant! roared to life
> as the flame rose through and
> our eyes recoiled from it.

The poem is intended to manifest a resurrection—all the more marvellous because it is made up of words, which are death. "The Pink Church" is nominally what I have called a "talking" poem; "Burning the Christmas Greens" is nominally a seeing poem. Yet how easily, for Williams, the one becomes the other! How easily that creative awareness toward which they lead becomes ritual! How naturally it takes its substance from matters associated traditionally with ritual—churches and Christmas greens! The poem has become a prayer; but he who prays, prays only to himself and that part of himself he can discover in his world.

Because Williams has wanted so much from poetry, he has proclaimed from the rooftops of the world the necessity of reconceiving its technique. Technique has meant for him only the "line" and a "workable metric"—as though the sole necessary condition for a poem were an adequate prosody.

> —Roy Harvey Pearce, "Williams and the 'New Mode'." *William Carlos Williams: A Collection of Critical Essays*, (Englewood Cliffs: Prentice-Hall, Inc., 1966): pp. 99-101.

BERNARD DUFFEY ON UNRESOLVED IMAGES IN THE POEM

[Bernard Duffey is the author of *Poetry in America: Expression and Its Values in the Times of Bryant, Whitman, and Pound* and *A Poetry of Presence: The Writing of William Carlos Williams*. He taught at Duke University. In this excerpt from a chapter that details Williams' use of the present image, Duffey argues that the images in the three-part narrative contribute to an understanding of the reality of religious experience precisely because they resist final definition.]

What this poet needs to attain any hold upon religious reality is a shift of technique of the kind present in "Burning the Christmas Greens." In that complex and beautifully proportioned poem, unresolved images allow him to focus upon the strangeness of religion, to enter it as his light will allow. Religion is present in the work simply as the season; it is observed as ritual even though no belief is present, and thus it can be examined as action, wholly unlike the praying machines of the monastery. The action is threefold: the house is decorated for Christmas and hence transformed; the difference at first is enjoyed; then it all grows tiresome and the greens are burned, but the new movement of the now-dry boughs causes a surprised recognition of continued transformation. Even in his own agnostic household, Christmas is the occasion of rebirth. Religion here, as in "The Catholic Bells," goes along with the life of the coral in which all are involved and, by the changes it signals, makes that life visible and present. There is no final attainment, only process and its attesting of the reality Williams finds in the presence informing so much of his work. Here, in contrast to "The Semblables," religion is real to the poet because bent to share in a life which otherwise it seems to turn away from.

> —Bernard Duffey, *A Poetry of Presence: The Writing of William Carlos Williams,* (Madison: University of Wisconsin Press, 1986): pp. 156-157.

PETER SCHMIDT ON THE POEM'S LYRIC TECHNIQUE

[This excerpt details Schmidt's view that the poem is both Williams' most important early lyric and the apex of his formal concerns at the time.]

The large historical cycles between Iron and Golden Ages, or Old Adam and New Messiah, are internalized and speeded up: the rebirth experienced in "Spring and All," like spring itself, is continually lost, found, and lost again. Williams' poem ends poised on the verge of awakening, looking backward toward winter yet foreseeing spring:

Now the grass, tomorrow
the stiff curl of wildcarrot leaf

One by one objects are defined—
It quickens: clarity, outline of leaf

But now the stark dignity of
entrance—Still, the profound change
has come upon them: rooted, they
grip down and begin to awaken
(*CP1*, 183)

"Burning the Christmas Greens" (1944) is an even richer drama-
tization of rebirth. With the possible exception of "The Descent," it
is the most important lyric Williams wrote in the 1940s, and it
demonstrates how he used the Precisionist techniques tested in his
shorter lyrics to construct a medium-length poem. Like "Chicory
and Daisies," it is a still life—but one that suddenly explodes into
flames, matter instantly transformed into energy. And as in
Williams' earlier still lifes, each detail is an Equivalent registered
within: the flames are "red as blood wakes / on the ash" (*CLP*, 16).
Between Williams' description of the moment of the burning of the
greens, however, he intersperses short narrative sequences showing
a family gathering and arranging the evergreen boughs, as well as a
tender but stark meditation on the meaning of their midwinter rite.
Williams had done something analogous at the end of "Queen-
Anne's-Lace," when he exchanged the frozen moment of the still life
for a leap forward in time ("empty, a single stem, / a cluster . . . / . . .
/ or nothing") (*CP1*, 162), and at the end of "Spring and All," which
trembles on the edge of both winter and spring. "Christmas Greens,"
however, audaciously uses such a vibrating structure for an entire
poem, rapidly shifting between a single, repeated spot of time cen-
tered on a still life and interpolated narrative sequences occurring
before and after that moment.

The first narrative sequence in the poem (lines 12–34) is a flash-
back in which Williams tells of a family gathering the Christmas
green during a "moment of the cold's / deepest plunge" and combining them with store-bought decorations. They build a make-
believe forest on the fireplace mantel, using the hemlock sprays and
some small white deer, perhaps made of china or porcelain. The narrator speaks for the whole group in third person plural, and details

are kept generic, so that the family's rite could take place any midwinter, in any American home. After describing this ritual, Williams then jumps forward in time again to the moment of burning, when, "their time past," the decorations are cracked apart and stuffed on the top of a "half burnt out / log's smoldering eye, opening / red and closing under them" (*CLP*, 16-17). As the family waits for them to catch fire, Williams' meditation returns to the past a second time (lines 41–55), not to describe gathering the greens but to meditate on the meaning of this midwinter ritual.

Williams stresses the pagan ritual behind the family's half-Christian, half-secular ceremony: greens forestall the cold by foretelling the arrival of spring. This section of the poem is in part a reworking of one of Williams' earlier (and best) pastoral poems, "To Waken an Old Lady" (1920). The "snow's / hard shell" and the birds' "plaintive, rallying cries" of "Burning the Christmas Greens" recall the setting of the earlier poem, but now the personification of the struggle of living creatures against winter is even more urgent. Williams turns what had been a birdsong tempering the winter wind into a man-made shelter: the boughs are "those sure abutments" and "a promise of peace, a fort / against the cold." The spiritual meanings that Williams is able to give these efforts are consequently more complex than in "To Waken an Old Lady"; gathering the greens symbolizes all human effort to reshape nature so that we may survive its harshness, from religious rituals to civilization's most advanced architecture.

Suddenly the greens burst into flame—and in the last five stanzas of the poem the mood shifts rapidly and becomes apocalyptic: "Transformed! / Violence leaped and appeared," and the branches are suddenly "Gone! / lost to mind // . . . / . . . in the contracting / tunnel of the grate" (*CLP*, 18). Yet as one world is destroyed, another appears; Williams transforms the ashes of the still-life greens into a view of our planet as it must have looked just after its creation:

> Black
> mountains, black and red—as
> yet uncolored—and ash white,
> an infant landscape of shimmering
> ash and flame
> (*CLP*, 18)

Williams is confident that his barren but brave new world may eventually be given human values, just as a newly created landscape is gradually colonized by plants. In fact, Williams' poem suggests that the twin worlds of the poem—ashes and evergreens, nature as desolate landscape and as a green world remade "to fill our need"—are doubles, twin images rapidly alternating between each other.

Williams does this brilliantly, by having the poem's last line, "the shining fauna of that fire," allude to a crucial earlier image, the white deer on the mantelpiece. By superimposing the two images, Williams creates a composite picture of the kind of creature that can live in the poem's double world. Such a creature, Williams tells us, must know that there is a time to fill our need for order and a time to expose ourselves to chaos—a time for gathering greens and a time for burning them. Man must repeatedly throw himself outdoors, out of the green world he constructs for himself, if his compulsion for shelter is to retain its integrity. This is why the poem constantly jumps back and forth in time: it is trying to teach us to live in both worlds. For Williams, his unnamed American family has this ability; they are both "lost" and "refreshed," symbolically bereft of home and excited by their discovery of a new world in which to live:

> breathless to be witnesses,
> as if we stood
> ourselves refreshed among
> the shining fauna of that fire.
> (*CLP*, 18)

The ending of "Burning the Christmas Greens" also alludes to "To Elsie" from *Spring and All*, both in its apocalyptic tone and in its repetition of crucial terms like *witness* and *shining fauna*. The earlier poem confronted chaos but despaired of ever being able to give it value; the poet remained alienated from his pastoral dream of perfection: "the imagination strains / after deer / going by fields of goldenrod" (*CP1*, 218). "Christmas Greens" is a revision, an answer to "To Elsie" and all the other mock pastorals in *Spring and All*, such as "Flight to the City." In it, Williams not only discovers "peasant traditions" that can substitute for the ones Elsie lost but also finds his own part to play in the ceremony. Significantly, those traditions are largely unconscious, continually changing, and thoroughly heterogeneous—an American melting pot of pagan rites, Old World

Christianity, and twentieth-century secular values. And at the center of this pastoral vision, celebrating the end of one year and the birth of another, stands the poet, truly the "happy genius!' of his household.

"Burning the Christmas Greens" thus opens for us the kernel, the heart of the heart of Williams' pastoral vision. Like earlier pastoral, especially Vergil's, it has a pronounced Messianic strain, prophesying the return of a Golden Age, of Adam to the Garden. But Williams' pastoral (like that of the Precisionists) is also a distinctively American version of the myth, reworking the meaning of the new world that is to be born. Although the return to harmony that Williams' representative American family experiences is temporary and provisional—next year they must symbolically repeat the rite of burning all they have built—the joyous conclusion of the poem envisions an ever-immanent rebirth of that Golden Age here and now, in the United States. The poem ends not merely with a glimpse of a new landscape but a Columbus-like discovery of an American Eden. Williams' Precisionist lyrics are thus poems about prophetic vision as well as the accurate recording of what is to be seen. Their conception of being "witnesses" to their age is hardly photographic or even merely optic, at least as those words are usually (and narrowly) used. Their pastoral vision has much in common with the *prospective* eye celebrated by Emerson and Whitman, particularly the Emerson of "Circles" and *Nature*. For this reason, references to vision play crucial roles throughout "Christmas Greens." The moment the greens catch fire is terrifying to watch: all "recognition" of what they were is lost (l. 4), and the family's eyes momentarily "recoil" from the sight (l. 59). Even more disturbingly, Nature's indifferent and destructive power in the poem is represented as a malevolent "smoldering eye" (l. 38) ready to destroy everything that mankind builds. The poem's prophetic pastoral vision of a new world must *stare down* this challenging gaze, transform its holocaust into a vision of hope.

—Peter Schmidt, *William Carlos Williams, The Arts, and Literary Traditions* (Baton Rouge: Louisiana State University Press, 1988): pp. 43-46.

"January Morning"

"January Morning" was published in Williams' collection *Al Que Quiere!,* a work that most critics agree was the poet's first major statement and important "new" contribution to letters at the time. In it, Williams develops some of his experimentation with line and, as Peter Schmidt has pointed out, begins to stretch away from the dramatic monologue and the lyric, which up until that point had dominated his work. At the same time, as Schmidt also points out (see excerpt below), Williams had read recent Cubist work on polyphony. Williams' use of multiple voices, characters, and styles would reach full maturity in *Paterson*, but "January Morning" is notable and often discussed because of its early example of Williams' use of polyphony.

The poem is subtitled "*Suite:*" to let readers know the parts to follow are interconnected and in a necessary series. The poem itself is delivered in fifteen sections that proceed in a roughly linear manner, telling the "story" of a January morning from the perspective of the individuals who experience it.

In the first section, the narrator himself places the poem squarely in Williams' familiar territory, this time in Weehawken. The narrator states that the heart can stir at the local church just as it does for Saint Peters, particularly if one has waited years to look on it again. In the years prior to the publication of *Al Que Quiere*, Williams had finished medical school and married, and had returned to Rutherford in 1912. It was the longest time he would ever spend away from his beloved hometown, and so the revelation of the first stanza and its celebration of the local convey a personal and vivid passion for what might otherwise be, on a cold January morning, far more austere and unwelcoming. As the narrator says "the beauties of travel are due to/ the strange hours we keep to see them:" and we know he is up early enough to see the light hit the domes of the Paulist Church in Weehawken.

It is clear in section II why he is up so early. He was prepared for an operation. It is postponed, but since he is out, he sees the probationers going to breakfast, as well as the gentlemen exiting from "basement entries" (section III), the sun "Streaking the tops of/ the irregular red houselets" (section IV), and the young horse (section V) and the "dirt colored men/ about a fire bursting from an old/ ash can" (section VI). In these sections, each a snippet of the eye or of the narrator's attention, he is noticing several different classes of person outside on the street. The class distinctions are noted in the description. The dwellings, not yet full houses, are "houselets." The gentlemen are "neatly coifed" and "middle aged," wearing signs of their sober intentions. The horse is the vigor of the morning, its "bared teeth and nozzle high in the air!" Even the fire of the dirt colored men is "bursting" from the ash can, such that even though their lot is recognizable, Williams infuses it with something more than only dejection. The fire itself is lively here, and perhaps something for which they are somewhat grateful on the cold morning. The enthusiasm of the narrator carries into section VII, where the car rails, blue "like the sky!" are "gleaming" and the link between the heavens and the terrestrial goings-on of the morning is made. It is an important link here, setting up the contemplative nature of the next few sections.

Section VIII starts with the drama of a dash and the use of the conjunction "and," just as the previous five sections do. The narrator thus divides the images while straining against the division with the breathless quality of each stanza's opening. But in section VIII, that boisterous voice shifts. The narrator celebrates the "rickety ferry-boat 'Arden'" and remarks at the irony of the name. Arden is a forested section of England wherein Shakespeare's fanciful *As You Like It* is set. The juxtaposition of the place and the ferry-boat with the same name underscores an important theme in the poem: the celebration and exultation in the activity that gives such color to a January morning. The narrator need not strain to make the connection; the boat itself is among "the great piers" and the "ever new river!" When the captain talks, it is to nearly cast a spell over the boat. He hollers for a Touchstone, to test the mettle of the boat, to follow gulls and "the ghost of the Half Moon/ to the North West Passage," both pseudo-mythical places rooted in reality, underscored by the very real locale of Albany. The captain's color in the scene is a voice of enchantment that presages the passages that follows in section IX, the most lyrical and imaginative of the poem.

In section IX, the narrator communes with the spirit of the sky over a river of ice crusts and brown waves and silver circlets. The use of alliteration and assonance heighten the quality of the voice here. The spirit of the sky is a "white gull with delicate pink feet/ and a snowy breast for you to/ hold to your lips delicately!" The image recalls the gulls that guide the boat, and the sky is no longer the "smoky dawn" of the first section. The rare spot of metaphor here, as well as the narrator's address to an undefined "you," make this section, ironically, perhaps the most direct message to readers. Of course, the "you" is revealed in the end to be the "old woman" for whom and to whom the poem is written. Still, the manner of address draws the reader in to the section, into the fanciful metaphors of flight and freedom, and to the ability to be both within and above the scene of the January morning. It is exultant.

Thus, the poet, or "young doctor," is "dancing with happiness" in section X. At the front of the boat, crossing the river, he sees in the harshness of ice and wind the images of summer. His seeing them is a way of linking the seasons in their natural splendor. The "ice crusts" are newly echoed in "shell-crusted ledges," and "the emerald eel-grass" is set away from the rest of the stanza, almost as a reach. In his reverie, the doctor then looks around him in section XI, and sees the "little peering houses" and the dawn rising "behind the moody water-loving giants of Manhattan." The very real skyscrapers here are made more with the metaphor of giants, and they are given the emotion of moodiness. The houses peer. The surroundings, which include the ferry, the basements, the ice, the prow, and the buildings, all inanimate, become a living environment. That they do in January is important, as it is a month that resonates with cold and death and slumber in the northeast.

But the more sober voice of section XII, with its perception of the botanical landscape and the doctor perceiving it, is subdued and, perhaps, even malevolent. Color is the important factor in the stanza; the rushes are yellow, the distant wood is a "purple and gold ribbon" that to the narrator, who "lie[s] there in contemplation," risks over-romanticizing. That he does so, and that some voice, be it his own inner rebuke or that of a greater narrator, recognizes this makes it the most cerebral and most complete perspective of the surroundings. The calm root of the scene, and the poet's emotions, lie there.

It is an important moment in the poem because it sets the mood for the following section.

Section XIII again addresses the "you" directly. It warns that one day the soul will be "out!/ —among the little sparrows/ behind the shutter." One day, performing just as mundane a task, fixing a chair or going to work, you will realize where your soul lies, just as the poet has during his routine ride on the ferry. In that light, his world has become more fanciful, real, exultant. But the poet must come back to the present at some point, and so section XIV reminds us: "flapping flags are at/ half mast for the dead admiral."

The final section tells the you, now the old woman again, that the poem was for her. Williams wanted, just as he did throughout his work, to write a poem "that you would understand." But, he warns, "you got to try hard." He is speaking in the vernacular English he assumes or knows to which the old woman is accustomed. His final explanation is a comparison of himself to the thrilling discovery of the world inherent in the image of the young girls on Park Avenue when they should be home in bed. He is not, then, seeing the world on the terms that most have accepted. He is being frivolous, risky, unconventional, and exuberant on the January morning in question. While he has written a poem he would like her to understand, he concedes that it will take a frame of mind, or a sympathy toward that frame of mind, to fully understand the voices and the visions he has arranged for her.

As in much of Williams' poetry, the overlooked and the static, the dead and the man-made become more. They become natural things precisely because he has found them and illuminated them within the world to which he has devoted his attention.

"January Morning"

PETER SCHMIDT ON THE POEM'S RESERVED POLYPHONY

[Schmidt's explication of the poem makes the case that while Williams is experimenting in Cubist polyphony, the poem is reserved in its use of the technique, even as it lays the groundwork for his future uses of the technique.]

Williams' first efforts to write poetry with a Cubist polyphony of voices began soon after he read Marius de Zayas' article linking polyphony and Cubism in *291* in March, 1915. At first, with "March" (1916) and "January Morning" (1917), Williams experimented with polyphony tentatively, as if he still felt dependent upon the dramatic monologue that he had used for so many of the poems he was assembling for publication in *Al Que Quiere!* in 1917. But with "Overture to a Dance of Locomotives" (1917) Williams confidently concluded the poem as Apollinaire might have done, by having the voices of people in a train station (in Williams' case, the newly opened Penn Station in New York City) interrupt the meditations of the poem's speaker.

In "January Morning," Williams' use of many voices is restrained, a matter of changes of inflection rather than of obviously different characters; the poem remains essentially a dramatic monologue unified by its voice but broken up into very short, fashionably Imagist sections. The poem is about a ferry trip Williams took home to New Jersey after apparently staying up all night on duty in a New York City hospital. The fifteen short sections of the poem, composed of things he waw and imagined on his way home, tend to separate into independent details and different moods, thus pulling against the centripedal forces that a monologue should maintain. The shortness of the stanzas and the incompleteness of the sentences further this fragmenting effect; the most common transition from one sentence fragment to the next is simply a dash and an and: "—and the worn, / blue car rails (like the sky!) /gleaming among the cobbles!" (*CP1*, 101). In addition, Williams uses the first person in only four out of seventeen sections and gives us few clues as to who is speaking and what action is taking place. All these aspects of the poem begin to displace the first-person speaker from the center of this monologue, unlike what happens in a classic monologue by Robert Browning or even any of those in Al Que Quiere!

This displacement may have been one reason why Williams sub-titled the poem "Suite." The name primarily refers to the collection of impressions that make up the poem but may perhaps also be taken to refer to the "suite" of tones in his voice. There is first the sober, reflective voice of the opening section, in which Williams stands the genre of the exotic travel narrative on its head by focusing on the local and the familiar. "I have discovered," the poet reports porten-tiously, that

> the domes of the Church of
> the Paulist Fathers in Weehawken
> against a smoky dawn—the heart stirred—
> are beautiful as Saint Peters
> approached after years of anticipation
> (*CP1*, 100)

Then there is the exclamatory voice that takes over the poem after the *I* disappears in Section II; it seems to be the voice not of a vet-eran traveler but of one experiencing the trip for the first time. It excitedly announces the details described in Section II through Vii with merely a dash and an *and* for each:

> —and from basement entries
> nearly coiffed, middle aged gentlemen
> with orderly moustaches and
> well-brushed coats
> (*CP1*, 101)

In the middle of Section VIII, the poem modulates again, as Williams leaves the city behind to board the ferry. Being on the open water increases his excitement, and instead of merely naming objects exuberantly, as he did before, in Sections VIII and IX he addresses them directly and uses extravagant figures of speech as if to portray the excitement of being on the open water. The ferry, christened the Arden, is changed by Williams into a dream ship piloted by Shakespeare's Touchstone, while the river's brown waves become adorned with "circlets of silver" and the sky is turned into a magical seagull with "delicate pink feet / and a snowy breast for you [the sea] to / hold to your lips delicately!" (*CP1*, 102).

In Section XI the more sober narrator of Section I returns, speaking as authoritatively as he did in Section 1, and on the same topic, too: "Who knows the Palisades as I do / knows the river breaks east from them / above the city" (*CP1*, 102–103). The emphasis here is on the importance of repeated, familiar experience, not the exclamatory revelations of the earlier sections. In Section XII, Williams' mood continues to calm; he describes the long yellow rushes on the approaching New Jersey shore as if they lay still, "in contemplation." The excitement of the city streets and the open water ebbs as the ferry ride nears its end.

Sections XIII and XIV deal with death, and for the first time Williams' voice is tired, caustic, ironic: "work hard all your young days / and they'll find you too, some morning / staring up under / your chiffonier at its warped / basewood bottom" (*CP1*, 103–104). This memory, perhaps recalling a corpse Williams attended that morning, appears without apparent reason—little that he sees in the landscape would seem to remind him of death. It may be that Williams' slowly fading exuberance prompts it. But the slightly somber mood of these lines contrasts markedly with the unrestrained joy of the earlier sections, or with the joy that returns in the codalike last section of the poem as Williams tells the story of his all nightter to his mother:

> Well, you know how
> the young girls run giggling
> on Park Avenue [in Rutherford] after dark
> when they ought to be home in bed?
> Well,
> that's the way it is with me somehow.
> (*CP1*, 103–104)

Cynic, giggling girl, young doctor, experienced old-timer who like Henry Thoreau or Whitman knows the joys of traveling close to home—all these characters seem to have bought passage with Williams on the ferry. The poem's strength is that it makes his monologue dramatic and varied. But Williams would only have to vary and to juxtapose these voices more assertively and he would begin moving away from the form of the dramatic monologue altogether.

—Peter Schmidt, *William Carlos Williams, The Arts, and Literary Traditions* (Baton Rouge: Louisiana State University Press, 1988): pp. 64-66.

WILLIAM MARLING ON THE POEM'S STRUCTURE OF TRIANGULATION

[William Marling is Professor of English at Case Western University. He is the author of *The American Roman Noir, Raymond Chandler, Dashiell Hammett,* and *William Carlos Williams and the Painters.* The essay discusses the act of sex and the resultant clarity following the act, and so looks at how Williams' poems mimic this tension in their structures. In his discussion of the poem in particular, he discusses how its core tension is released in the final images.]

Williams can be said to step on the stage of American poetic tradition with "January Morning" (1917) from *Al Que Quiere.* It is also a poem that deploys the pattern of triangulation, out-of-body forward motion, interruption, and a resulting new realm of detail. The poem opens on the ferry to Manhattan. As if remembering the "Mole" in Geneva, Williams glances back at his social milieu on the Jersey shore:

> the domes of the Church of
> the Paulist Fathers in Weehawken
> against a smoky dawn—the heart stirred—
> are beautiful as Saint Peters
> approached after years of anticipation.
> (*CP1*, 100)

The domes crowning the transepts and mixed with spires provide the vertical element of triangulation. Sections II through VII deliver precise scenes and sharp details set in the New York City to which the poet travels, at which he has not arrived. They anticipate the future, as Kandinsky advised. This prevision is as important as their appearance in the poem. The poet knows what he will see, evidence of what

Heidegger termed *dasein*, an intentionality with relation to "being in the world."

In Section VIII Williams' field of vision contracts to the ferryboat, lingering on allusions that connote his conventional intent: "Arden," the quest for "the North West Passage—and through!" In Section IX his glance falls to the water—"the sky has come down to you"—and his visual narrowing renders most acutely the sensation of disembodied forward motion.

"The young doctor is dancing with happiness" as the tenth section commences. He is "alone / at the prow of the ferry." In this purely experiential realm, he "notices" the textures of "curdy barnacles" and "broken ice crusts." He contrasts the winter scene with its opposite, but he keeps sensual summer at a distance. The fourth term, the spatial enlargement or cold detail, may not be achieved until Williams turns on the fulcrum, makes his perceptual pivot—and in this poem, the explicit posting of the turn follows the vertical and horizontal triangles.

It happens that in Section XII "long yellow rushes bending / above the white snow patches" make "an angle" that replicates the angle of the prow the poet occupies. Such explicit doubling designates the moment of contact, the fulcrum, but here the poet will not "turn" until he probes the stasis of his form:

> what an angle
> you make with each other as
> you lie there in contemplation.

Williams then proceeds to a profane vertical: in the constricted space of the prow, he contemplates the claustrophobic view of someone dead

> staring up under
> [a] chiffonier at its warped
> bass-wood bottom.

The spatial reversal produces a dramatic effect: the first view is *down* on crossing yellow rushes that evoke the illusion of "the distant wood," the second view is *up* only inches at a "warped" wood bottom.

As in *The Autobiography*, Williams imagines an intruder. Here it is his English grandmother, aged and approaching death, the "devil" in the prosaic sense because she undid the domesticating efforts of Williams' mother (Mariani presents the evidence). Williams equated her life with obstinacy, intransigence, a limited depth of field; in a Yale manuscript, "The Three Letters," written around 1921, Williams developed a comparison between his grandmother and the baroness, as "interrupting" women. Williams' valorization of the intruder (and "the flapping flags," a vertical motif, at "half mast for the dead admiral") sets up the opposing intensity of the horizontal, out-of-body motion toward the horizon of

> the young girls [who] run giggling
> on Park Avenue after dark
> when they ought to be home in bed.

If they were "home in bed," sensation would not pile up as formlessly as it does "giggling / on Park Avenue after dark." This is a poem that makes the round," that brackets detail at its center, ending on motion, on a reopening of vision onto the "corridor to a clarity" that produces it. The poem achieves part of its sense of giddiness by this reversal of visual strategies for containing motion and detail.

Although Williams was too curious a craftsman to dwell on one pattern, the spatial template of "Postlude" and "January Morning" is found in other poems, especially "The Attic Which Is Desire." The title of this poem, standing grammatically parallel to the first line, introduces the subject and the spatial matrix of triangulation, but takes a colder view of the potentiality the form holds than do the previous poems. This triangle is

> the unused tent
> of
>
> bare beams
> beyond which
>
> directly wait
> the night
>
> and day—
> Here

from the street
by

```
* * *
* S *
* O *
* D *
* A *
* * *
```

ringed with
running lights

the darkened
pane

exactly
down the center

is
transfixed

(*CP1*, pp. 325–26)

No "loud eaves" rattle here. This triangle is "unused," an "attic" in which desire becomes merely "bare beams." Clear vision has been socially marginalized by expectations of a "SODA." Williams does not linger: the point is that the shape is reduced to eidetic bareness; it is a vessel of potentiality. This poem concerns itself with *interruption*, with what Peter Schmidt has termed "the machinery of stimulating desire." The poet's prevision passes through the attic peak, an anticipated height whose inexpressibility he indicates by aposiopesis and descends to the opposed point of view. The view up / the view down, as in "January Morning," has a linear element, a "corridor to a clarity" that squares the triangular and leaves the poem running outward. "SODA" will light, presumably, in a moment, but it leaves the reader at a state of attention. Interruption is anticipated, not achieved. This technique, borrowed from contemporary painting, especially the ready-mades of Marcel Duchamp, privileges the "erotic atmosphere." Williams adapts the technique to his own spatial biography: to the initially triangular, barren attic, perceived from within, he opposes the subsequent "darkened / pane" whose light is imminent. This corridor will produce a clarity, but the critical interruption has not yet occurred. The reader must "see" beyond the edge of the page. The diction that gives rise to this effect is cold and winterish: "darkened pane," "down the center," "transfixed." If we await the word to appear longer than meet, we may realize that "soda" is not simply sweet, but also sodium carbonate, a bitter leavening agent.

Of the many other poems in Williams' oeuvre amenable to this reading, none is better known than "The Yachts." It is widely remarked for the way in which the preservation of the poem's "false start" leads to the poet's discovery of his real subject.

> Now the waves strike at them but they are too
> well made, they slip through, though they take in canvas.
>
> Arms with hands grasping seek to clutch at the prows.
> Bodies thrown recklessly in the way are cut aside.
> It is a sea of faces about them in agony, in despair
>
> until the horror of the race dawns staggering the mind
> (*CP1*, p. 389)

The discovery of the faces in the waves, across which the prow of the yacht cuts, is not simply thematic. It is also a spatial resolution consonant with the pattern of triangulation described above: Williams considers first the vertical triangles of the sails and fails to find a race (that is, an "interruption"), then turns to the horizontal. In the waves he finds material he had ironically "passed over," the faces, perhaps, of the baroness, Hartley, and others, cut by the "craft" to which he sacrificed them. Only seeing "as with waves above me" is Williams in command of the second perceptive matrix that makes the poem.

> —William Marling, "'Corridor to a Clarity:' Sensuality and Sight in Williams' Poems." *Twentieth Century Literature* 35 (1989): pp. 292-294.

PETER HALTER ON THE MOVEMENT FROM MELODIC POEM TO SYMPHONIC POEM

[Peter Halter is Professor of American Literature at the University of Laussanne. His other books include *Katherine*

Mansfield und die Kurzgeschichte, William Shakespeare: Measure for Measure, and *The Revolution in the Visual Arts and the Poetry of William Carlos Williams.* Halter shows that "January Morning" is an early example of how Kandinsky's ideas of melodic structure and symphonic structure inspired Williams, and how it satisfied the poet's yearning for formal experimentation beyond free verse.]

Williams's first attempt at writing a poem that moves, in Kandinsky's terminology, from the "melodic" to the more complex "symphonic" form is "January Morning" (*CP1*, 100). The subtitle "Suite" could refer to Kandinsky's "constructional tendencies" and indicate that the poet is trying to achieve the composite form of a suite by a succession of more or less self-contained "melodic" imagistic units. Some of these units can be related to one another by the principle of opposition—as theme and countertheme, so to speak—juxtaposing, for instance, inertia and movement, dreariness and exhilaration, constraint and liberation:

XIII

Work hard all your young days
and they'll find you too, some morning
staring up under
your chiffonier at its warped
bass-wood bottom and your soul—
out!
—among the little sparrows
behind the shutter.

XV

. . . .
Well, you know how
the young girls run giggling
on Park Avenue after dark
when they ought to be home in bed?
Well,
that's the way it is with me somehow.

Other units could be called equivalents: that is, they are similar in one respect and dissimilar in another; musically one could call them variations of a common theme:

II

Though the operation was postponed
I saw the tall probationers
in their tan uniforms
                    hurrying to breakfast!

III

—and from basement entries
neatly coiffed, middle aged gentlemen
with orderly moustaches and
well brushed coats

This overall structure is often repeated within the individual units, as in the following one where the images of winter in the first part of the unit and summer in the second are related by contrast as well as by analogy:

X

The young doctor is dancing with happiness
in the sparkling wind, alone
at the prow of the ferry! He notices
the curdy barnacles and broken ice crusts
left at the slip's base by the low tide
and thinks of summer and green
shell-crusted ledges among
                    the emerald eel-grass!

Even on the level of the smallest details the organizing principles of analogy and contrast can be detected. Thus the soft movement of the "exquisite brown waves" with "long circlets of silver moving over [them]" in section IX has its equivalent in the "emerald eel-grass" of the next section, while on the level of contrast in both instances the harmony evoked by the gentle movement of these things and the play of light over them is juxtaposed with the harshness of the "crumbling ice crusts among [them]" (IX) and the shell-crusted ledges" (X).

—Peter Halter, *The Revolution in the Visual Arts and the Poetry of William Carlos Williams* (New York: Cambridge University Press, 1994): pp. 28-29.

[John Lowney is Assistant Professor of English at St. John's University. He is the author of *The American Avant-Garde Tradition: William Carlos Williams, Postmodern Poetry, and the Politics of Cultural Memory* as well as a number of critical articles. In this section, Lowney not only links Williams to his poetic forbears, most notably Whitman and Wordsworth, he shows how the poem moves beyond the elder poets' solipsism and narrative and into a "polyphonic" work with elements that highlight the performance aspects of poetry, and how its use of apostrophe renders the poem immediate and confrontational. Halter goes on to claim that "January Morning" is a forbear to Williams' later long and cyclical poems, and to a host of postmodern poetics.]

Williams takes up the question of Whitman's importance for modern American poetry in "America, Whitman and the Art of Poetry" (1917). In this essay he claims that Whitman is "our rock, our first primitive. We cannot advance until we have grasped Whitman and then built upon him." If Whitman represents the "pinnacle" of American poetry, he also stands as an "edifice" whose imposing presence must not only be "grasped" but resisted. Williams indicates his own strategy for dealing with Whitman's colossal presence:

> The only way to be like Whitman is to write unlike Whitman. Do I expect to be a companion to Whitman by mimicking his manners? I might even so please some old dotard, some "good grey poet" by kow-towing to him; but not to Whitman—or if I did please Whitman I would not please myself. Let me at least realize that to be a poet one must be himself!
>
> What have I done now! "Be himself?" What the devil difference does it make to anyone whether a man is himself or not as long as he write good poetry. "Be a Whitman, if you will, only please, if you love your kind, *don't write like Whitman.*"

The dialogical process of self-correction—the abrupt transition from "one must be himself" to "What have I done now!"—suggests one method for writing unlike Whitman. The Whitmanesque "I," which enacts the nationalist vision of assimilation, becomes the "I" that sustains its "divisions" or that "fidgets with point of view." In positing a split between "being" and writing, Williams opens the possibility for incorporating the style and idealism of Whitman, while still experimenting with new poetic forms and more realistic modes of presenting modern subjects. Williams resists Whitman's idealizing nationalism, but he appropriates his insistence on the "American language" to focus on "local" linguistic structures and "local" experience. We can trace this process of being a Whitman, but writing unlike him, most explicitly in "January Morning."

"January Morning" recalls "Crossing Brooklyn Ferry" in its language and in its subject, as it records the poet's journey across the Hudson between Manhattan and New Jersey. However, the structure of this poem, a "suite" of fifteen short sections in various rhetorical modes, looks forward to the cubist polyphonic collage of such poetic sequences as *Spring and All*, *The Descent of Winter*, and *Della Primavera Trasportata al Morale* more than it looks back to Whitman. "January Morning" begins with the poet's localization of the "beauties of travel," as he argues that the familiar can be aesthetically appreciated when perceived in unfamiliar conditions:

> I have discovered that most of
> the beauties of travel are due to
> the strange hours we keep to see them:
>
> the domes of the Church of
> the Paulist Fathers in Weehawken
> against a smoky dawn—the heart stirred—
> are beautiful as Saint Peters
> approached after years of anticipation.
> (*CP1*, 100)

Using a familiar Wordsworthian trope to describe a defamiliarized scene, this vision of Weehawken nevertheless affirms the aesthetic value of New World spontaneity, contrasted to the more rational Old World "anticipation." The poem then proceeds to describe what the poet sees in the early morning urban streets with a sequence of descriptive predicate clauses, each beginning with "and," following the initial "I saw." The paratactic syntax and oratorical free verse rhythm resembles Whitman, but there is a significant difference: each of the seven predicate clauses is a separately numbered stanza.

This series of self-contained vignettes transforms Whitman's catalog into a series of imagist lyrics. The first half of "January Morning" sustains a coherent, realistic narrative, but the numbered sequence of vignettes produces the effect of a series of snapshots. This sequence can be viewed more mimetically as interrupted glimpses recorded from the poet's train-window vantage point. This method of juxtaposing images becomes more complex when the narrative itself becomes fragmented, as the poem begins to juxtapose varying speech acts:

> —and the rickety ferry-boat "Arden"!
> What an object to be called "Arden"
> among the great piers,—on the
> ever new river!
>
>   "Put me a Touchstone
> at the wheel, white gulls, and we'll
> follow the ghost of the Half Moon
> to the North West Passage—and through!
> (at Albany!) for all that!"
> (*CP1*, 102)

This stanza deviates from the realistic description of the previous stanzas, as its reference to Shakespeare's *As You Like It* imparts an aura of romance to the ferry journey. This reference to Williams's frequently cited exemplar for timeless literary excellence is supplemented by references to voyages that are historically and geographically closer to Williams. The "ever new river" may be read as an echo of Heraclitus or as a metaphor for the experience of modernity, but Williams's affirmation of his own local knowledge, his ability to read this "ever new river," also evokes Twain's Mississippi River pilots. The reference to the *Half Moon* reaffirms such realistic use of detail as Twain's, as romantic or even fantastic as it sounds, for it recalls a voyage by Henry Hudson himself, the explorer whose name imparts a historical continuity to the "ever new river." However, Williams takes up where Hudson left off ("to the North West Passage—and through!"), for the *Half Moon* was Hudson's ship for a voyage of exploration that he abandoned at Albany. This reference to Hudson's voyage toward the North West Passage furthermore evokes Whitman's affirmation of American exploration and expansion, especially the optimistic nationalism of "Passage to India." Finally, this passage marks a transition from the first-person narrative to a mixed mode of address. Among these modes is the mode of address that appears in quotation marks in the extract; it is a problematic mode for modern poetry, the mode of apostrophe. The use of apostrophe here and later in "January Morning" makes this poem's invocation of Whitman more parodic than imitative.

The poet quotes himself when he tells the "white gulls" to "Put me a Touchstone / at the wheel," thus distancing himself from the apostrophic act. However, the poem goes on to address the "Exquisite brown waves" in language reminiscent of "Crossing Brooklyn Ferry." This apostrophic mode plays a crucial role in Williams's transformation of the Whitmanesque lyric "I" in "January Morning." Jonathan Culler has argued that the use of apostrophe epitomizes the lyric's difference from other genres. Apostrophe functions in post-Enlightenment poetry as a strategy for overcoming the alienation of subject from object. Invoking the orphic power of poetry to make objects responsive forces, apostrophe enacts a process of subject–object reconciliation by making the object function as a subject. Unlike narrative, lyric apostrophe locates events in the present, removing the opposition of absence and presence from empirical time and locating it in discursive time. Apostrophe thus produces a fictive, discursive event, rather than the representation of an event. However, Culler also notes that apostrophe, as the "sign of a fiction which knows its fictive nature," can also be read as an act of radical interiorization or solipsism. The rarity of usage of apostrophe in modern poetry can be attributed to anxiety about such solipsism.

By interrupting the narrative description of "January Morning" with an apostrophic address, Williams dramatizes the performative aspect of poetry. But the apostrophic passages of this poem so resemble Whitman that they function almost as quotations, as texts inserted into a cubist collage, rather than as the lyric speaker's performative act. The stanzas following the poem's several apostrophic passages suggest that apostrophe is deceptively solipsistic. Rather than transforming objects into subjects, apostrophe transforms the speaking subject into an object. For example, the stanza following the address to the waves begins:

> The young doctor is dancing with happiness
> in the sparkling wind, alone
> at the prow of the ferry.
> (*CP1*, 102)

Although on its surface a celebration of lyric solitude, this passage replaces the lyric "I" with the more distanced, more objectified "young doctor," who proceeds to reject the present "curdy barnacles and broken ice crusts" for a more nostalgic vision of this same landscape in summer. The next instance of apostrophe, this time addressed to "Long yellow rushes," has a much more alarming sequel:

> XII
> Long yellow rushes bending
> above the white snow patches;
> purple and gold ribbon
> of the distant wood:
>   what an angle
> you make with each other as
> you lie there in contemplation.
> XIII
> Work hard all your young days
> and they'll find you too, some morning
> staring up under
> your chiffonier at its warped
> bass-wood bottom and your soul—
> out!
> —among the little sparrows
> behind the shutter.
> XIV
> —and the flapping flags are at
> half mast for the dead admiral.
> (CP 1, 103)

The stanza following the personified "rushes" is itself apostrophic, but the voice is disembodied and sinister in its authoritative tone (the "you" addressed is not only the poet but a typical "you" that includes the reader). The sudden change of mood from the meditation on natural beauty to the admonition about death corresponds with the abrupt shift of address. As an objectified speech act, one whose speaker and addressee cannot be determinately located, this stanza implicitly critiques the previous apostrophic passages. If the apostrophic act imbues the lyric speaker with the authority of poetic tradition—in this case the authority of the Whitman tradition—this authority itself is portrayed as a fiction. The fictional act of apostrophe is here associated not only with solipsism but with death. If lyric poetry exists only within the bounds of the fictional, of the aesthetic, of poetic tradition, if it has no social function in everyday life, then indeed the poet "alone / at the prow of the ferry" becomes the "dead admiral."

"January Morning" ultimately escapes the solipsism of postromantic lyric poetry by grounding the colloquy of speech acts within a conversation, a conversation elusively situated in the poet's locality:

> All this—
> was for you, old woman.
> I wanted to write a poem
> that you would understand.
> For what good is it to me
> if you can't understand it?
> But you got to try hard—
> But—
> Well, you know how
> the young girls run giggling
> on Park Avenue after dark
> when they ought to be home in bed?
> Well,
> that's the way it is with me somehow.
> (*CP1*, 103–4)

This final address to "you, old woman" is frequently associated with Williams's paternal grandmother, Emily Dickinson Wellcome, but according to his recollections it was actually addressed to his mother, whose multilingual background and thwarted aspirations of becoming an artist played a formative role on Williams's literary identity throughout his career. "January Morning" subtly situates Williams's construction of "national" literary descent within this "local" filiation. The poem's final reference to "Park Avenue" reiterates this double construction, as "Park Avenue," a main street of Rutherford, evokes the better-known Manhattan address. This reference bridges Whitman's New York with Williams's Rutherford, but it also establishes Williams's position for a "localist" avant-garde within the New York avant-garde. While acknowledging the difficulty of the poem's oblique juxtaposition of imagistic stanzas, the conclusion opens the process of interpreting the poem into a playful, rather than laborious, act. As an objective correlative for the poem's complex of feelings, the conclusion liberates the reader from the quest for symbolic correspondences, proposing instead a play of modes and images whose structure anticipates Williams's longer poetic sequences in the 1920s.

—John Lowney, *The American Avant-Garde Tradition: William Carlos Williams, Postmodern Poetry, and the Politics of Cultural Memory* (Lewisburg: Bucknell University Press, 1997): pp. 33-38.

CRITICAL ANALYSIS OF

"These"

The title is also the start of the verse in this poem, and the opening
lines are a bleak and savage vision, almost an indictment: "These/
are the desolate, dark weeks/ when nature in its barrenness/ equals
the stupidity of man." The tone is not the only unusual aspect of the
piece. "These" was never published in a stand-alone collection,
although it was included in the "Recent Verse" section of 1938's
Complete Collected Poems of William Carlos Williams. As
Williams' career was gaining speed, he was becoming increasingly
concerned with culture, politics, and the state of the world. While his
poetry was, we now know, informed by such concerns, it was rare
for them to take center stage in a work. For that reason alone,
"These" would be worth a look. But the poem also offers a preview
of Williams' later decision to pay greater attention to formal matters.
The opening statement of a relationship equates the scarcity of a
winter landscape with the lowest mental state of humans. The stanza situates the poem in winter. The narrator, the thought behind the
poem, sees that barrenness equals stupidity and brutishness. There is
nothing to offer in such a state, nothing can grow. Because we know
that winter eventually ends, there is the possibility for rebirth and
change. But it will be a while before that happens here. Instead, the
time of year is reiterated in the next line. It is December—"The year
plunges into night"—and a time of despondency, when the heart
goes to a place without the heavens, as described in line 8. We understand the absolute depth here due to the repetition of "plunge." It
does have light, "a peculiar light as of thought" but it is not the daz-
zling celestial stuff of "sun, stars, or moon" and their burden of stories.

   It is "thought// that spins a dark fire—" and Williams' lyricism
here conveys the imaginary and inexplicable nature of the fire. It
occurs in an "empty, windswept place," a place uncluttered, and a
place deep within. The fire "whirls upon itself" and in so doing
becomes thought. To the poet, it is a particularly self-aware thought.
The person so involved becomes aware of "nothing/ that he knows."
The line break makes one sense an unwritten "the" which might

come before "nothing." It is the awareness of the utter lack, the very absence of something, which the man knows. The echo of this idea can be heard in the work of Stevens and Hemingway in pieces written and made famous years before Williams sat down to write this poem, and such nothingness was an often used theme of the Modernists. "These" has Williams now attacking it in the fourth stanza.

However, in this case, the sense of the nothing becomes very particular, more so than in previous pseudo-mystical references by other writers. The narrator qualifies that it is not "loneliness/ itself— Not a ghost" but it is tangible enough to be held, even, as the poem says, "embraced." The nothing is to be cherished in a nearly physical way. It is partly emptiness and despair, as the poem says, but it has context. Throughout these qualifying stanzas (lines 14-17), the poet is also using dashes, enjambment, and sparse syntax to slow our understanding, to make our comprehension as gradual as it is for the man in the poem. The poem overall is rather ponderous in its tone, but here particularly it slows the reader to ensure that the point comes through. Hence, the parentheses: "(They/ whine and whistle)." Those who perceive the nothing also hear the cries of its components.

The stanza to follow puts the moment of realization in larger context: "the flashes and booms of war,/ houses of whose rooms/ the cold is greater than can be thought," and the places are where such barrenness begins. The scenes evoked are ones of bereavement: a time of war, an empty home. In the description of the unused furniture, Williams conveys the powerful sense of desolation evoked in the poem's first line. Here, he uses things to convey the idea. (One of Williams' most famous and philosophical lines, first expressed in the 1927 poem "Paterson," is "No ideas but in things." The description of the furniture—"the beds lying empty, the couches/ damp, the chairs unused—is a good example of William's philosophy at work.) When in the following stanza, in line 25, he exhorts the reader to "Hide it away somewhere" the "it" refers to the nothing and the knowledge of it. Here the poem begins to turn. The desolation and even despair is to be "out of the mind" so that it "gets roots" and will grow. In this way, the barrenness has something reborn, which means that stupidity does not remain that way. By embracing the loneliness and loss, out of the sight of all, and letting it grow to more, one gains power. After all, as the poem says, "In this mine they come to dig—all." Those who know capitalize on such feelings and work to make something of them.

The poem asks, "Is this the counterfoil to sweetest/ music?" The break at sweetest makes the thought linger a moment. The nothing is the opposite to sweetness, a source of strength perhaps. But when music is then associated with sweetest, the poem presents a paradox. The next line continues the inquiry, whether or not the nothingness is the source of poetry that is melancholy, poetry that remembers the days of a running clock, for instance, on noticing the clock has stopped. Is the lament the source of art? Is it when things stop that we find the power to recall their beauty? Does it take loss, or the drying of a lake, for us to imagine "the sound of lakewater—splashing—that is now stone" or some other deprivation for us to appreciate things? Again, things are at the fore for this idea. Williams is asking in a larger way why those things that he notices as a poet are not noticed and appreciated by those that come in contact with them daily. Why, he asks, is the realization of our love for things predicated on our losing them?

CRITICAL VIEWS ON

"These"

DENIS DONOGHUE ON THE POEM AS EVIDENCE OF WILLIAMS'
INTELLECTUAL POWER

[Denis Donoghue was a Fellow of King's College,
Cambridge, and is the author of *The Third Voice,
Connoisseurs of Chaos: Ideas of Order in Modern
American Poetry,* and *Words Alone.* Donoghue is now
Henry James Professor of English and American Letters at
New York University. Donoghue includes the poem with
others of Williams' as examples to drive home the point that
Williams was indeed a poet after larger ideas, contrary to
the opinion of his detractors. Donoghue contends that
Williams sought to develop "a grammar of American cul-
ture."]

The core, the source, the root: this is the concern of *In the American
Grain,* many of the *Essays,* of *Paterson,* and *The Great American
Novel.* The people of *Paterson* move around, without motive, inar-
ticulate, because they do not understand themselves, not under-
standing their origin, their source. Williams is concerned to show
that there is something under the soil, roots which (understood) give
new life and meaning. Hence his unacademic resuscitations of
Columbus, Cortez, the founding of Quebec, the *Mayflower,* Aaron
Burr; his inspired cribbing from Cotton Mather, from Franklin's
Information to those who would remove to America, from William
Nelson's *History of the City of Paterson and the County of Passaic.*
Hence his devoted elucidation of James Otis, Patrick Henry, William
Bartram, Crèvecoeur, Freneau, his hymns to Jefferson, Franklin,
Washington and (in his own world) Alfred Stieglitz. But history does
not explain everything; there is still, as part of the core, the irrational,
the things we have to include to represent all we do not understand.
So, in *Paterson,* Williams inserts a few letters which have nothing to
do with the 'story', but which are qualitatively apt, standing for the
impalpable *something* which inhabits the real. It all fits in.

But where? And how? Many readers of Williams have felt that he is too short on organization, on large-scale manipulations issuing from a coherent penetration of experience. True, his manipulations often seem to be fragmentary epiphanies (as in 'The Red Wheelbarrow') and yet I should be surprised to find that they are not determined by some Idea, some Universal, of which they are partial enactments. Recall that it was Williams who wrote:

> It is hard to say what makes a poem good, but if it is not in the detail of its construction, it is in nothing. If the detail of the construction is not to the smallest particular distinguished, the whole poem might as well be thrown out.

It is difficult to reconcile this with the great big lumpkin who, we are told, wouldn't be caught dead in the company of an idea. There is on my side the evidence of such poems as 'Tract', 'These', 'Dedication for a Plot of Ground', 'The Lonely Street', 'A Coronal'. There is Williams' life-long devotion to craft, to measure, to the resources of speech, to a redeeming language. And behind all this there is his vigorous idea of culture. Just listen to him talking about it:

> The burning need of a culture is not a choice to be made or not made, voluntarily, any more than it can be satisfied by loans. It has to be where it arises, or everything related to the life there ceases. It isn't a thing: it's an act. If it stands still, it is dead. It is the realization of the qualities of a place in relation to the life which occupies it; embracing everything involved, climate, geographic position, relative size, history, other cultures—as well as the character of its sands, flowers, minerals and the condition of knowledge within its borders. It is the act of lifting these things into an ordered and utilized whole which is culture. It isn't something left over afterward. That is the record only. The act is the thing.

This is not the writing of a fuddy-duddy; these are deep matters, to be ignored at our peril, and Williams refuses to ignore them. In fact, what he has undertaken to provide (in poems, essays, fiction, drama) is a grammar of American culture; American because that is what he has at hand and knows best and cares most about, not because he thinks it the richest culture ever achieved. I do not claim that it is a perfect grammar; it omits too much, despite its profusion. For one thing, to place beside it Eliot's *Notes towards the Definition of*

Culture is to see that Williams' grammar lacks a focal religious perspective; and I am of Eliot's party in this respect. But I revere Williams—and Stevens—for what they have carved out from what they had in hand; without evasion or falsification. A Grammar of Culture without benefit of Clergy: I have no temptation to sneer.

—Denis Donoghue, "For A Redeeming Language." In *William Carlos Williams: A Collection of Critical Essays*, (Englewood Cliffs: Prentice-Hall, Inc., 1966): pp. 125-126.

PETER SCHMIDT ON MELANCHOLY AND THE ODE

[In the excerpt, taken from a longer consideration of the poem as an ode, Schmidt unveils the several "ghosts" that haunt the poem; the ghosts are either formal matters or Williams' own memories.]

"These," like most recent penseroso lyrics, draws upon both the positive and negative attributes of melancholy. In the first lines of the poem, Williams' mood is angry but articulate. In the middle stanzas, as he recites his catalogue of loss and destruction, his anger deepens and his voice becomes broken apart by semi-colons and dashes, stops and starts, and negatives negating each other. The saturnine qualities of melancholy, however, begin to modulate into Williams' own American version of *furor divinus* just after the lines on the abandoned homes quoted above. If those lines mark the point of Williams' deepest descent into despair, the poem's last four stanzas imply that a turn upwards may be possible in the distant future. I take this transition to the last four stanzas to be the crux of "These," and one of the most difficult passages in all of Williams' work.

Williams breaks off his description of the empty houses with a dash and then leaps to a new stanza, as if trying resolutely to distance himself from the barren scene. Take this hell-fired vision of flames, bombs, and abandoned homes, he pleads, and

> Hide it away somewhere
> out of the mind, let it get roots
> and grow, unrelated to jealous
>
> ears and eyes—for itself.
> In this mine they come to dig—all.

Because the mind of a poet is jealous of what it apprehends and continually wants to remake the external world in its own image, Williams seeks to restrict this process by "hiding" his private despair within general, universal language that allows multiple meanings rather than jealously guarding a single, personal one. Thus in the above lines the "it" that must get roots and grow is deliberately left ambiguous; the pronoun may refer to the houses, emptiness, despair, or the nameless "ghosts" in turn.

The phrase "hide it . . . out of the mind" may also be taken to describe the very process presently occuring in the poem, as Williams' vision of barrenness and violence is expelled out of his imagination and set down on paper. If so, that explains the poem's next line: "In this mine they come to dig—all." Once given form, Williams' vision is available to all who come to decipher it, and the meaning of Williams' visionary plunge changes; the poet's descent into despair potentially becomes a discovery of wealth, of the resources to be mined from the mind.

By describing truth as something "hidden" yet available to all, the "mine" image prepares us for the stoical confidence of the poem's close, so different from the bitter declamations of its opening lines. The concluding two and one-half stanzas of "These" juxtapose a set of rhetorical questions about the poem's dark prophecies. Each has the phrase "the source of poetry" (i.e., Williams' "mine" of despair) as its referent, and each is to be answered with an emphatic "yes":

> If this the counterfoil to sweetest
>
> music? The source of poetry that
> seeing the clock stopped, says,
> The clock has stopped
>
> That ticked yesterday so well?
> and hears the sound of lakewater
> splashing—that is now stone.

Here Williams embraces his many ghosts proudly; they are all he has. He forms his ghosts both from private memories (the clock upon a home's mantel) and his knowledge of Nature herself, who over vast spans of geologic time fills in a lake and forms sedimentary rock. These ghosts become "the source of poetry" not because they let the mind retreat into nostalgia but because through them the mind is able to contain both past and present, presence and absence. The poet's prodigious feats of memory, moreover, suggest new strength. His mind spans both clock time and natural history, retaining all: both the vanished sounds of the lakewater and the present silence of the rock exist for him in the *present* tense. Williams thus casts a cold eye on both the homes that we build and all that nature makes. He watches as all are unmade. The poem's closing is as dramatic as its opening, but it is subtler drama. Its tone is steady and stoical, not angry and contradictory—all life is to be turned to stone; all music, to silence. If the lines are filled with despair, therefore, they are also compact with potential strength. Such strength represents, I think, a renewed faith that the poet's poetic powers will eventually return, although they seem barren now. In "These" Williams thus unobtrusively blends the sound and fury of *furor melancholicus* with a trust in patience, perseverance, and humility that is associated with the spiritual labors necessary to *furor divinus*.

The stoic mixture of optimism and pessimism at the conclusion of "These" is reassuring, especially in view of the feverish anger of the poem's opening. It seems a moment of calm, of quiet questioning—a prelude to a return of imaginative power. Williams' strength is analogous to Shelley's in the last lines of "Mont Blanc" and to Stevens' in "The Snow Man." Stevens' skeptical man of snow, like the speaker of "These," is composed out of "nothing," a "cold greater than can be thought," and he courageously acknowledges that the imagination may negate itself as violently as any force in nature. But of all the modern penseroso poems shadowing "These," Keats's Hyperion poems (1818–19), especially "The Fall of Hyperion," exert the strongest influence, stronger even than Milton's "Il Penseroso" or Stevens' "Domination of Black." The influence of Keats's melancholy poems about paralysis and failure is the most hidden or repressed, however. It can be certainly felt in "These" only in the poem's cryptic last lines about water turning to stone, when Williams echoes prominent tropes that Keats uses. And Williams' sudden recollection of Keats could not occur at a more difficult time. Williams involuntarily opens himself to Keats's ghost just after he has contained the presence of Stevens and Milton and just when he is trying to contrive a close for his poem.

—Peter Schmidt, "These:' Williams' Deepest Descent," *William Carlos Williams Review*, IX (1983): pp. 74-90.

[In the excerpt, Sullivan describes how the poem is in fact "told" from the perspective of a persona, and not through omniscient narration.]

In Williams' 1938 poem "These" (*Selected Poems,* 90–91) we find no use of first-person singular per se, but we read in the second stanza after the poet announces that the "year plunges into night" (l. 4):

> . . . the heart plunges
> lower than night
>
> to an empty, windswept place
> without sun, stars or moon
> but a peculiar light as of thought
>
> that spins a dark fire—
> whirling upon itself until,
> in the cold, it kindles
>
> to make a man aware of nothing
> that he knows, not loneliness
> itself— (ll. 5–15)

In "the heart" and "a man" we readily perceive allusions to an unnamed "I" whose presence throughout is confirmed in stanza eight when the poet casually uses the first-person-plural pronoun as he refers to "people gone that we loved" (l. 22).

The difficulties of the poem remind us of Steiner's third level of difficulty, the kind the critic calls "tactical" because it results in a "rallentando" effect to slow the reader down in the name of deepening the experience of comprehension (35). But such difficulty is not an impasse and is overcome without too much delay in "These" because of the firm assurance of understanding provided by the sense of a first person controlling the poem's events. The constant shifting of subjects and of second and third-person pronouns referring to those subjects, as well as the deliberate use of vague pronoun reference, create a good example of the effect Steiner compares to "moiré", . . . the meaningful but unstable and reticulating patterns of shot silk." Elaborating, Steiner continues: "There is a distinct sense in which we know and do not know, at the same time. This rich undecidability is exactly what the poet aims at. It can be made a hollow trick . . . Or it can serve as a true tactical difficulty, forcing us to reach out towards more delicate orderings of perception. It is, simultaneously, a subversion and energizing of rhetoric drawing attention . . . to the inertias in the common routine of discourse" (40). Even in the last four stanzas of "These" where Williams is most ambiguous, shifting as he does to the imperative mood and addressing an unnamed second person, the "you" is an indirect way of saying "I," for without too much strain we can imagine he is addressing himself.

—Janet Sullivan, "Encountering the Unicorn: William Carlos Williams and Marianne Moore," *Sagetrieb* 6:3 (1987): pp. 148-149.

Works by

WILLIAM CARLOS WILLIAMS

Poems, 1909.

The Tempers, 1913.

Al Que Quiere!, 1917.

Kora in Hell: Improvisations, 1920.

Sour Grapes, 1921.

The Great American Novel, 1923.

Spring and All, 1923.

GO GO, 1923.

In the American Grain, 1925.

A Voyage to Pagany, 1928.

A Novelette and Other Prose (1921-1931), 1932.

The Knife of the Times and Other Stories, 1932.

The Cod Head, 1932.

Collected Poems 1921-1931, 1934.

An Early Martyr and Other Poems, 1935.

Adams & Eve & The City, 1936.

White Mule, 1937.

Life along the Passaic River, 1938.

The Complete Collected Poems, 1938.

In the Money: White Mule—Part II, 1940.

The Broken Span, 1941.

The Wedge, 1944.

Paterson (Book One), 1946.

Paterson (Book Two), 1948.

The Clouds, Aigeltinger, Russia, &, 1948.

A Dream of Love: A Play in Three Acts and Eight Scenes, 1948.

Selected Poems, 1949.

The Pink Church, 1949.

Paterson (Book Three), 1949.

The Collected Later Poems, 1950; revised, 1963.

Make Light of It: Collected Stories, 1950.

A Beginning on the Short Story [Notes], 1950.

Paterson (Book Four), 1951.

The Autobiography, 1951.

The Collected Earlier Poems, 1951.

The Build-Up: A Novel, 1952.

The Desert Music and Other Poems, 1954.

Selected Essays, 1954.

Journey to Love, 1955.

I Wanted to Write a Poem, ed. Edith Heal, 1958.

Paterson (Book Five), 1958.

Yes, Mrs. Williams: A Personal Record of My Mother, 1959.

The Farmers' Daughters: The Collected Stories, 1961.

Many Loves and Other Plays: The Collected Plays, 1961.

Pictures from Brueghel and other poems, 1962.

Paterson, books 1-5 and notes for book 6, 1963.

Imaginations, edited by Webster Schott, 1970.

The Embodiment of Knowledge, ed. Ron Loewinsohn, 1974.

A Recognizable Image: William Carlos Williams on Art and Artists, ed. Bram Dijkstra, 1978.

Yvan Goll, Jean sans Terre: Landless John, translated by Williams, Lionel Abel, Clark Mills, and John Gould Fletcher, 1944.

Pedro Espinosa (Don Francisco de Quevedo), *The Dog & the Fever,* translated by Williams and Raquel Hélène Williams, 1954.

William Carlos Williams

Ahearn, Barry. "Williams and H. D., or Sour grapes." *Twentieth Century Literature* 35 (Fall 1989): pp. 299-309.

Baker, Tony. "The comedian as the letter 'n': sight and sound in the poetry of William Carlos Williams." *Journal of American Studies* 18 (April 1984): pp. 89-103.

Barry, Nancy K. "The fading beautiful thing of Paterson." *Twentieth Century Literature* 35: (Fall 1989): pp. 343-63.

Berry, Eleanor. "William Carlos Williams' triadic-line verse: an analysis of its prosody." *Twentieth Century Literature* 35 (Fall 1989): pp. 364-88.

Blackmer, Corinne E. "Writing poetry like a 'woman'." *American Literary History* 8 (Spring 1996): pp. 130-53.

Bremen, Brian A. *William Carlos Williams and the diagnostics of culture.* New York: Oxford University Press, 1993.

Bremen, Brian A. "'The radiant gist': 'the poetry hidden in the prose' of Williams' Paterson." *Twentieth Century Literature* 32 (Summer 1986): pp. 221-41.

Breslin, James E. B. *William Carlos Williams, an American artist.* Chicago: University of Chicago Press, 1985.

Buelens, Gert. "The American poet and his city: Crane, Williams and Olson; perceptions of reality in American poetry (1930-1960)." *English Studies* 73 (June 1992): pp. 248-63.

Callan, Ron. *William Carlos Williams and transcendentalism: fitting the crab in a box.* New York: St. Martin's Press, 1992.

Castellito, George P. "A taste of fruit: the extended hand in William Carlos Williams and imaginative distance in Wallace Stevens." *Papers on Language & Literature* 28 (Fall 1992): pp. 442-50.

Conarroe, Joel. *William Carlos Williams' Paterson: language and landscape.* Philadelphia: University of Pennsylvania Press, 1970.

Crawford, T. Hugh "Paterson, memex, and hypertext." *American Literary History* 8 (Winter 1996): pp. 665-82.

Crawford, T. Hugh. *Modernism, medicine & William Carlos Williams*. Norman: University of Oklahoma Press, 1993.

Cushman, Stephen. *William Carlos Williams and the meanings of measure*. New Haven: Yale University Press, 1985.

Dickie, Margaret. *On the modernist long poem*. Iowa City: University of Iowa Press, 1986.

Dickie, Margaret. "Williams reading Paterson." *ELH* 53 (Fall 1986): pp. 653-71.

Diggory, Terence. *William Carlos Williams and the ethics of painting*. Princeton: Princeton University Press, 1991.

Diggory, Terence. "The reader in Williams and Brueghel: Paterson 5 and The adoration of the kings." *Criticism* 30 (Summer 1988): pp. 349-73.

Dijkstra, Bram. *Cubism, Stieglitz, and the early poetry of William Carlos Williams: the hieroglyphics of a new speech*. Princeton: Princeton University Press, 1978.

Doyle, Charles *William Carlos Williams and the American poem*. New York: St. Martin's Press, 1982.

Dunn, Allen. "Williams's liberating need." *Journal of Modern Literature* 16 (Summer 1989): pp. 49-59.

Flinn, Anthony. *Approaching authority: transpersonal gestures in the poetry of Yeats, Eliot, and Williams*. Lewisburg: Bucknell University Press, 1997.

Fredman, Stephen. "Williams, Eliot, and American tradition." *Twentieth Century Literature* 35 (Fall 1989): pp. 235-53

Funkhouser, Linda.; O'Connell, Daniel C. "'Measure' in William Carlos Williams' poetry: evidence from his readings." *Journal of Modern Literature* 12 (March 1985): pp. 34-60.

Gonzalez, Lisa Sanchez. "Modernism and Boricua literature: a reconsideration of Arturo Schomburg and William Carlos Williams." *American Literary History* 13 (Summer 2001): pp. 242-64.

Goodridge, Celeste. "Private exchanges and public reviews: Marianne Moore's criticism of William Carlos Williams." *Twentieth Century Literature* 30 (Summer/Fall 1984): pp. 160-74.

Graham, Theodora R. "Williams, Flossie, and the others: the aesthetics of sexuality." *Contemporary Literature* 28 (Summer 1987): pp. 163-86.

Gregory, Elizabeth. *Quotation and modern American poetry: imaginary gardens with real toads.* Houston: Rice University Press, 1996.

Hoagland, Tony. "On disproportion." *Parnassus: Poetry in Review* 19 (1994): pp. 110-27.

Johnston, Walter E. "Style in W. C. Williams and Charles Ives." *Twentieth Century Literature* 31 (Spring 1985): pp. 127-36.

Juhasz, Suzanne. *Metaphor and the poetry of Williams, Pound, and Stevens.* Lewisburg: Bucknell University Press, 1974.

Kinnahan, Linda A. *Poetics of the feminine : authority and literary tradition in William Carlos Williams, Mina Loy, Denise Levertov, and Kathleen Fraser.* New York: Cambridge University Press, 1994.

Klink, William. "Permanence and change in the Paterson, New Jersey, of William Carlos Williams." *Journal of American Studies* 21 (Dec. 1987): pp. 422-6.

Koehler, Stanley. *Countries of the mind: the poetry of William Carlos Williams.* Lewisburg: Bucknell University Press, 1998.

Kutzinski, Vera M. *Against the American grain : myth and history in William Carlos Williams, Jay Wright, and Nicolas Guillien.* Baltimore: Johns Hopkins University Press, 1987.

Lacey, Paul A. "'To meditate a saving strategy': Denise Levertov's religious poetry." *Renascence* 50 (Fall 1997/Winter 1998): pp. 17-32.

Lawson, Andrew. "History and/or the abyss: William Carlos Williams's Asphodel." *Contemporary Literature* 33 (Fall 1992): pp. 502-27.

Lloyd, Margaret Glynne. *William Carlos William's Paterson: a critical reappraisal.* Rutherford: Fairleigh Dickinson University Press, 1980.

Lowney, John. "The 'post-anti-esthetic' poetics of Frank O'Hara." *Contemporary Literature* 32 (Summer 1991): pp. 244-64.

MacGowan, Christopher. "Williams' last decade: bridging the impasse." *Twentieth Century Literature* 35 (Fall 1989): pp. 389-405.

MacGowan, Christopher J. *William Carlos Williams's early poetry: the visual arts background.* Ann Arbor: UMI Research Press, 1984.

Markos, Donald W. *Ideas in things: the poems of William Carlos Williams.* Rutherford: Fairleigh Dickinson University Press, 1994.

Markos, Donald W. "Memory as a new 'present' in Williams' later poems." *The Southern Review* 24 (Spring 1988): pp. 303-13.

Matthews, Kathleen D. "Competitive giants: satiric bedrock in book one of William Carlos Williams' Paterson." *Journal of Modern Literature* 12 (July 1985): pp. 237-60.

Mazzaro, Jerome. *William Carlos Williams: the later poems.* Ithaca: Cornell University Press, 1973.

Mester, Terri A. *Movement and modernism : Yeats, Eliot, Lawrence, Williams, and early twentieth-century dance.* Fayetteville: University of Arkansas Press, 1997.

Monteiro, George. "The existence of an American Venus: William Carlos Williams versus Henry Adams." *Journal of Modern Literature* 20 (Winter 1996) pp. 248-53.

Moore, Patrick. "William Carlos Williams and the modernist attack on logical syntax." *ELH* 53 (Winter 1986): pp. 895-916.

Moore, Patrick. "Cubist prosody: William Carlos Williams and the conventions of verse lineation." *Philological Quarterly* 65 (Fall 1986): pp. 515-36.

Morris, Daniel. *The writings of William Carlos Williams: publicity for the self.* Columbia: University of Missouri Press, 1995.

Mota, Miguel M. "'It looked perfect to my purpose . . .': William Carlos Williams' contact with the Spanish." *Journal of Modern Literature* 18 (Fall 1993): pp. 447-59

North, Michael. "The sign of five: Williams' The great figure and its background." *Criticism* 30 (Summer 1988): pp. 325-48.

Poole, Robert. "Robert Frost, William Carlos Williams, and Wallace Stevens: reality and poetic vitality." *CLA Journal* 36 (Sept. 1992): pp. 12-23.

Qian, Zhaoming. *Orientalism and modernism: the legacy of China in Pound and Williams.* Durham: Duke University Press, 1995.

Quinn, Sister M. Bernetta. *The Metamorphic Tradition in Modern Poetry.* New York: Gordian Press, 1955.

Radloff, Bernhard. "Name and site: a Heideggerian approach to the local in the poetry of William Carlos Williams." *Texas Studies in Literature and Language* 28 (Summer 1986): pp. 140-63.

Rapp, Carl. "William Carlos Williams and the modern myth of the Fall." *The Southern Review* 20 (January 1984): pp. 82-90.

Riddel, Joseph N. *The inverted bell : modernism and the counterpoetics of William Carlos Williams.* Baton Rouge: Louisiana State University Press, 1974.

Rogoff, Jay. "Pound-foolishness in Paterson." *Journal of Modern Literature* 14 (Summer 1987):pp. 35-44.

Rosenthal, M. L. "Is there a Pound-Williams tradition?" *The Southern Review* 20 (April 1984): pp. 279-85.

Sayre, Henry M. "American vernacular: objectivism, precisionism, and the aesthetics of the machine." *Twentieth Century Literature* 35 (Fall 1989): pp. 310-42.

Sayre, Henry M. *The Visual Text of William Carlos Williams.* Urbana: University of Illinois Press, 1983.

Steinman, Lisa Malinowski. *Made in America : science, technology, and American modernist poets.* New Haven: Yale University Press, 1987.

Stoicheff, R. Peter. "Against 'an easy lateral sliding': William Carlos Williams' early poetry of differentiation." *American Poetry* 5 (Spring 1988): pp. 14-23.

Strom, Martha Helen. "The uneasy friendship of William Carlos Williams and Wallace Stevens." *Journal of Modern Literature* 11 (July 1984): pp. 291-8.

Townley, Rod. *The Early Poetry of William Carlos Williams.* Ithaca: Cornell University Press, 1975.

Walker, Jeffrey. *Bardic ethos and the American epic poem: Whitman, Pound, Crane, Williams, Olson.* Baton Rouge: Louisiana State University Press, 1989.

ACKNOWLEDGMENTS

Walker, David. *The Transparent Lyric: Reading and Meaning in the Poetry of Stevens and Williams* © 1984 by Princeton University Press. Reprinted by Permission of Princeton University Press.

Virgin and Whore: The Image of Women in the Poetry of William Carlos Williams by Audrey Rodgers © 1987 by McFarland & Company. Reprinted by Permission.

William Carlos Williams, The Arts, and Literary Traditions by Peter Schmidt © 1988 by Louisiana State University Press. Reprinted by Permission Louisiana State University Press.

William Carlos Williams and Alterity: The Early Poetry by Barry Ahearn © 1994 Cambridge University Press. Reprinted by Permission.

The Revolution in the Visual Arts and the Poetry of William Carlos Williams by Peter Halter © by Cambridge University Press. Reprinted by Permission.

Apocalypse and After: Modern Strategy and Postmodern Tactics in Pound, Williams, and Zukofsky by Bruce Comens © 1995 by University of Alabama Press. Reprinted by Permission.

The American Avant-Garde Tradition: William Carlos Williams, Postmodern Poetry, and the Politics of Cultural Memory by John Lowney © 1997 by Bucknell University Press. Reprinted by Permission.

William Carlos Williams: A New World Naked by Paul Mariani © 1981 by W.W. Norton and Company. Reprinted by Permission.

The Art of Poetry: Cummings, Williams, Stevens by Stephen E. Whicher © 1982 by Aquila Publishing. Reprinted by Permission.

William Carlos Williams and Romantic Idealism by Carl Rapp © 1984 by Brown University Press/University Press of New England. Reprinted by Permission.

"Encountering the Unicorn: William Carlos Williams and Marianne Moore," by Janet Sullivan © 1987 by *Sagetrieb*. Reprinted by Permission.

Themes and Ideas